ACCLAIM FOR *WHAT DO WE MAKE OF BACH?*

John Harbison has for decades been an inspired conductor of Bach cantatas, so it is not surprising that he has now written a superb small book revolving around Bach's music. Nothing could be more intense and moving than Harbison's brief accounts of various musicians associated with the great composer, or more lucid and instructive than his notes on individual works.

— Michael Fried, author of *Promesse du Bonheur*

In this fascinating collection of biographical sketches, essays, and program notes, Bach is the common thread, but in the end, the book is about far more than Bach. Through the lens of Bach, Harbison gives us a memoir of his evolution as a composer and performer, and offers a personal history.

—Richard Griscom, Head, Albrecht Music Library, University of Pennsylvania

In *What Do We Make of Bach?* the wise, witty, surprising, and infinitely touching portraits of friends, family, and colleagues (sometimes embodied in the same person), eloquent essays, and illuminating notes on Bach cantatas make up the autobiography we couldn't possibly have predicted. These fragments from a life devoted to music, and especially to Bach, actually add up to a whole and very rich life.

—Lloyd Schwartz, author of *Little Kisses* and *Music In - and On - the Air*

Written in the light of half a century of studying and performing Bach, Harbison's book – part memoir, part composerly meditation – offers valuable, eloquent insights into the journey of an essential American composer.

— James Primosch, Professor of Music, University of Pennsylvania

In these wonderfully personal, poetic, illuminating sketches and essays, John Harbison wears his erudition (I hesitate even to use such a weighted word) so lightly as to cause us to experience his subjects, with the central link of Bach's music, as a pleasant, albeit substantial, conversation among good friends. The depth of Harbison's knowledge is everywhere evident, but more importantly we begin to understand Bach's work as a living, breathing model for our musical and artistic selves.

—Robert Kirzinger, composer and Boston Symphony Orchestra annotator

WHAT DO WE MAKE OF BACH?

Portraits, Essays, Notes

JOHN HARBISON

Edited by
SARAH SCHAFFER

ARS Nova, LLC

Madison, WI

First published in 2018 by
ARS Nova, LLC • Publisher
Post Office Box 620254
Middleton, Wisconsin 53562
www.arsnovallc.com

Madison, WI

ISBN 978-1-7325097-0-2

Library of Congress Control Number: 2018953138

Grateful acknowledgement is made to Michael Fried for permission to include
"The Cave," to the Bach Archive Leipzig, and to Staatsbibliothek zu Berlin –
Preußischer Kulturbesitz, Musikabteilung mit Mendelssohn-Archiv for permis-
sion to reprint the Bach manuscript excerpts that illustrate this volume.

Edited by Sarah Schaffer
Published by ARS Nova, LLC, Middleton, Wisconsin
Designed by Andrée Valley, Madison, Wisconsin
Printed and bound in the U.S.A. by Thomson-Shore, Inc., Dexter, Michigan

Bach, Cantata BWV 162, Ach! ich sehe, itzt, da ich zur Hochzeit gehe, No. 3,
"Jesu, Brunnquell aller Gnaden" (aria for soprano and continuo). Original
obbligato lost, alternative version composed by John Harbison, 2018.

Contents

CANTATA NOTES

Joh. Seb. Bach

INTRODUCTION

*T*he title came first, *What Do We Make of Bach?*

This was in 2012, followed by some music for orchestra. Later, a suggestion to include Bach's main instrument, the organ. I began writing an extended program note, thoughts collecting around that title, *What Do We Make of Bach?*

Bach as a meeting point.

Bach as a measuring point.

Encounters—with people I have known, Bach as a magnet.

Encounters—with Bach's music, often part of my extended work as Principal Guest Conductor with Emmanuel Music, Boston.

Around, within his music a fellowship forms, a society engaged in making and doing, never simply honoring and preserving.

Bach, not as a monument but as a demanding, volatile presence, right in our ear.

THE CAVE

" . . . We are like blind fish in a Kentucky cave.
We have no eyes because there is no light,"
He said turning away, conducting Bach.

— Michael Fried

WHAT DO WE MAKE OF BACH?

WHAT DO WE MAKE OF BACH?

E. H. HARBISON

*M*y father was a Reformation historian, but also a good amateur musician. He played the piano. I remember mostly Bach, Debussy, and Gershwin. These composers were an influence on his youthful composition, which included a movement for violin and piano. When I was studying violin I used to play it with him. Later he composed many songs for Princeton University Triangle Club shows.

He might have wanted to be a musician— at concerts he gravitated to Scheide, Sessions, Cone, who seemed to regard him as well-versed. He knew a lot of music, much of it by memory. I got the impression his parents thought the arts to be inconceivable as *a life*. From their vantage point in business and philanthropy, even a university professorship was risky and bohemian.

When he wrote home from the Lawrenceville School that he had become very excited by reading Karl Marx, his mother's chauffeur appeared, weary from a two-day drive over dusty roads, to bring him home to Pittsburgh.

Among Jinks Harbison's favorite pieces to play were the Bach Schübler Chorales, arrangements for organ of six pieces from cantatas, which he knew in an adaptation for piano by Ferrucio Busoni. The one he played most, and which I often asked him to repeat, was the chorale prelude for tenors from Cantata 140, *Wachet Auf.*

He very kindly wrote out a simplification of the piece since I was avid to try it. I still have this very artfully made version and vividly remember puzzling it out with wonder, at the age of six.

It has interested me to try to compare my impressions of it then with impressions from later encounters. To my surprise, they don't seem to differ much, except in the language used for description.

As a young musician I would have noticed first the attractiveness of the florid melody. I would also have found pleasure in the striding bassline, pulsing so much more slowly than the melody. There was also a third element, coming in and out, something I might also have heard as a tune, but broken into segments, with a shape and bearing that suggested a special importance.

Even when very young, I loved the fact that all three of these tunes were different from each other. Even very young, playing them separately, I noticed that the third tune, whose presence was more scarce than the others, had . . . it had . . . some "advantage" over the others.

Here, literally stumbling at the edge of a great principle, Bach's strict-against-free Chorale practice, I am unable to say accurately what more a six-year-old could perceive about this piece. But I can hazard that in slowly practicing these separate elements, and painstakingly sounding them together, I was sustaining a crash course in counterpoint, as well as a quick immersion in the world of hierarchic musical character. In assigning hieratic musical roles to these three melodies, Bach in a very short space draws on stark differences of contour, activity, even point of historical origin.

The more I played this piece, in the difficult simplification my father had made (mainly compressing registers for small hands), I understood that a lot depended on *when* the third tune came in. In the first section, which repeats, its appearances seemed prepared, set up. Later on, when some of its phrases are very short, its entrances were more surprising, I had to work to remember the timing.

One of the entrances of the third tune just sounded wrong every time I played it.

This is the one I came to love the most.

Somewhere in the learning of this piece, especially in discovering that "wrong" entrance, I realized I wanted to be a composer. Bach's chorale-principle, present also in pieces which do not quote chorales but which nevertheless construct a hierarchy of subject matter, a "given" and a "less given" element — this way of organizing musical thought has always been home base for my compositional map. Years later, conducting the whole of Cantata 140 many times, it has been an endless delight to reconfirm that the *when* of the chorale is elevated to a stunning level of suspense and variety, proposing parallel possibilities for that "wrong" choral entrance I'd noticed so long ago in the tenor movement.

If you want to take an insider's ride in just a corner of Bach's mind (this is a little like my football expert friends exhorting me to just watch the left guard in the middle of the line on a running play), listen to the opening chorus of BWV 140, attending entirely to the entrance-relationships of the chorale (sopranos) and the three lower choral parts. Each placement turns out to be deliberately unlike the others.

I remember my father's office wall, portraits of Luther and Erasmus, the stone steps in his building worn down by the tread of teachers before him. After making another little transcription of a Bach piece and, when I was eleven, teaching me the changes of "Night and Day," verse and all, I don't remember him showing me much about the music he loved, the road he set me on. I think of the last time we played his violin piece, just before I switched to viola, sophomore year of high school, already noticing, a little sadly, places it could have been composed better.

You still wish your father could teach you everything.

The year before he died, and already very ill, he stood diffidently in the back of the hall for a run-through of a *Psalm for Soprano and Organ* I had just written. It was 1963, my last student year.

Speech was already very hard for him, smiling was not. I think he said, "You'll be all right."

Johann Sebastian Bach. Schübler Chorale, Cantata 140. Wachet auf ruft uns die Stimme; org; BWV 645. Staatsbibliothek Berlin: SA 4719.

Helen Abrahamian

*O*ur basic duo pieces were the Bach gamba sonatas. We played them all through school, with the special ensemble agreement siblings can have. I remember when I finally knew my part so well I could truly listen to her, the calm inwardness of her playing.

We played the G minor the night before we left for Mississippi, for our father, who could no longer speak and could barely move.

Part of the sound of growing up was the complete cello literature sounding somewhere in the house, always grounded by the six Bach suites, including always our mutual favorite concerto, the Schumann, the character of which represented her perfectly (the character which makes it both the least played and most distinguished of cello concertos).

Helen had the disadvantage of perfectionism, which haunted and scarred her brief life, as her various psychiatrists would learn. She was always the good child, the one who sang "O Holy Night" dressed as an angel, standing on a piano at the Christmas pageant. The one who got only A's, first in the class, who always phrased her cello pieces modestly and authentically, who learned French so easily, who looked and spoke with wit and tact. And most of the time she was miserable, nourishing a fierce resentment toward her parents which emerged with fury later on.

It was all summarized by the photo from her fifth birthday: riotous, laughing friends circling a cake, and a desperate, crying Helen.

Being, looking, acting perfect was costing her. There were some signs of rebellion. Her most intense teenage boyfriend was the furtive, hypersensitive, acutely introverted son of a Princeton physicist. They inhabited a silent mysterious duo-world of the misfit, strangely innocent. My first experience of absolute injustice was overhearing a phone call from the young man's father to my father: "You keep that crazy whore of a daughter away from my son." Professor Harbison, as disturbed as I've ever seen him, went to Helen, warned her to be vigilant, but pledged to affirm and protect her connection to her young boyfriend.

While we were in Mississippi, our father died. Helen and I flew back, received a ritualistic, terrifying review of his last hours from my mother, attended the service and, grateful for our engagement in another life-changing set of events, immediately boarded a plane back to Jackson. Two things happened. The plane lost pressure and flew the last hour at very low altitude. And we were seated with Bayard Rustin, already our hero in the movement. We wanted to know as much as he would tell us about his work, especially the March on Washington.

He found out we were musicians. He wanted to talk about Bach.

Helen was a founding member of the DaCapo Chamber Players, and had a great reputation as a player of new music. She had a strong presence in the New York music scene when she was found to have breast cancer. She decided to move, with her husband, the historian Ervand (Jed) Abrahamian, to have more family support. We formed a chamber ensemble, Seraphim, and she did much beautiful playing in this period, especially a great Schubert E-flat Trio with Rose Mary Harbison and Robert Levin, coached by Rudolf Kolisch.

But as her cancer moved to the bone, with great pain, a lot of other things mattered—the fate of her beautiful Seraphim 'cello, her relentless pursuit of self-help therapies, her determination to be physically active. And also ravenous anger at her fate, much of it absorbed by one of her devoted caregivers, Rose Mary Harbison.

I was always surprised by her unconditional love. I had been in early years an insufferable, teasing, superiority-crowing brother, but in the last hour she offered me an amazing gift. We talked about *what* was after death, what might remain. She had gathered courage. She knew I was writing a piano quintet. I agreed to have some music she would like in it. She went further: "Put some messages in there that are only for me."

John Harbison. Piano Quintet (1981); V. Elegia.

Harbison Heptet, 1951. L-R: Alan Shepard, trumpet; John Harbison, piano; Peter Smyth, drums; Tommy Shope, sax; Tommy Artin, trombone

TOM ARTIN

*T*om Artin arrived in Princeton from Bloomington when we were starting third grade. He lived right across the street. For the first few years I learned from him what an amazing, shining place Bloomington was, how everything was better there, how sometime they would all go back. He began turning up regularly at breakfast, presumably to walk to school, but he really had his mind on our breakfast, at which he looked longingly, until my mother would say, "Tom, would you like to have some of what we're having?" to which he always quickly replied, "Yes thanks I would," and devoured it like a starving dock worker.

Tom's father and mother were both mathematicians, his brother and sister were already headed that way, but music was central to the family. His father was organizing them into a baroque ensemble, himself on flute or keyboard, Karen on cello, Michael on violin, and Tom—well, Tom was already hooked on the trombone. This was only one of his early black-sheep behaviors. The family soon moved from our street, Aiken Avenue, to a grandly proportioned, marvelously cavernous manse at the top of a one-way street, Evelyn Place, in which Emil Artin's baroque organ held a central place in the vestibule.

It was a few years later that Professor Artin interrupted our Dixieland jam session, myself on his organ, Tom on trombone. He materialized (we thought the house was empty) in a heavy wool suit, vest and tie, bare feet, and brief case, on his way to work at 11 p.m. The Princeton mathematicians were famous for their nocturnal habits, the lights of Fine Hall blazing, alone, through the small hours of the morning. Emil Artin fixed me with an exasperated look. "About my son I had already given up, but from you I would expect something better."

At that moment I had no idea why he might expect something better from me, but Tom later informed me that it was known to his father that I was studying and composing longhair music, a wonderful term which lost currency after the Beatles Era.

On the music rack of the organ sat Bach's B minor Organ Prelude. Emil Artin gestured to it, very soberly. *"That* is the music I would wish to bring to your attention." The two chastened youths to whom he was speaking were not bold enough to mention that the music on the organ rack already held their attention. We already recognized parallels between the counterpoint in a Bach Chorale Prelude and the ideal Dixieland front-line. Fifty years later, playing together at the Token Creek Festival, we found ourselves still lost in admiration for both.

Our library, high school afternoons, was the local record store. Incredibly enough, they let you take records into a booth and try them out. Every few weeks, one of us would buy one. Sometimes we continued to try out one of our favorites for weeks. Unless the booths were full, our education continued, unharrassed, unedited. Those long afternoons we studied with the early contrapuntists: Louie, Wild Bill, Max, Ruby, Edmund, and Vic.

The band we formed at age eleven, Harbison's Heptet, mainly played Dixieland standards; our junior high school principal believed it was "not the best, but the loudest" band he had ever heard. As we continued to play that music, the rock era dawned. Tom and I fiercely upheld jazz, with the handwriting on the wall.

Alternating sets with a slick new rock band at a high school dance, actually opening for them, such that we were slinking away as they began their triumphant last set, we noticed that all their amplifiers plugged into a central cable. As we disappeared, one plug was pulled—then the satisfying sound of a deafening roar becoming tiny metallic plinks, the satisfying sight of slick jackets diving toward the outlet. But outside in the dark, realization, at fifteen, that our historical moment in mass culture was gone.

The other cultural strand, the north German counterpoint, Bach through Wagner, was absorbed at home. Tom's father, the great Heidelberg mathematician, like so many distinguished intellectuals driven out of Germany, was steeped in German culture, never abandoned it. (He eventually accepted the German government's lavish reparations offer to return to his post in the 1960s.)

My father's field was Reformation history, and everything in the house—the Dürer and Holbein reproductions, the stacks of Bach in the music cabinets—made me wonder why we weren't "Lutherans." His political crisis, the attempt by the campus McCarthyites to hunt him out of his job, while no parallel to the Artin experience, left a mark.

Our house on holidays was a haven for émigrés from the Institute for Advanced Studies, whose stories were a political education. Both of our families were in the center of the action in the Princeton Plan, New Jersey's first mandated school desegregation. In 1963 Tom was at the March on Washington, hearing King's address and taking the photos that were published in book form fifty years later. In 1964 Rose Mary Harbison and I were at Tougaloo College near Jackson, Mississippi, part of the Freedom Summer. These themes were still being heard when Tom wrote

The Wagner Complex, fearless in its investigation of the sources of Wagner's anti-Semitism. They drive many of my pieces: *Between Two Worlds, Abu Ghraib, Four Psalms.*

Playing jazz together each summer from 2006-2013 was a chance for me to marvel at Tom as Renaissance man. He is a supreme jazz trombonist, but also an imaginative, original photographer (as was his unforgettable earth-mother mathematician mother). He translates professionally, from German and Swedish. His musical activities include arranging, as well as organizing and promoting groups from duo to big band. And in the Wagner year 2013, he is embraced as an important contributor to the vast literature on one of our inexhaustible sacred monsters.

Framing all of this is a very knowledgeable devotion to Bach, whose music he continues to practice and study, as we did on Aiken Avenue when we were still, in my mother's phrase, "insufferable little know-it-alls."

In the official photo of Harbison's Heptet Tom sits directly below a bookshelf holding the decapitated bust of Beethoven, proudly displaying his drawing of Kilroy on his plastic hat mute. He looks alert and mischievous. Ready to rehearse some southern-fried north German counterpoint.

Hanns-Martin Schneidt

*W*hen I got to Berlin in 1960 I immediately began looking for Bach cantatas. It was probably my harpsichord teacher Sylvia Kind who steered me to Hanns-Martin Schneidt. I met him at the Hochschule for an interview, and soon found myself riding the S-Bahn to distant Spandau my second week in Berlin, on a Thursday night. The trip took over an hour. As it became increasingly rural, as darkness fell, we passed a grim sprawling fortress. A stranger seated across from me, identifying me correctly from my shoes, said, in correct American, "Spandau Prison. Rudolf Hess. The only prisoner, fifteen years." There was one light visible. I pictured Hess—alone, half-mad, imagining the Third Reich still existed. The date on the preface to the score of tonight's cantata "1942"—less than twenty years.

At the Spandau station singers from the choir of the Johannesstift, a small theological school, met me to guide me to the rehearsal. The station was brightly lit, their faces brightly lit. There were three of them; their fresh enthusiasm would become familiar, as would the source of the light in their faces. One of them I can conjure effortlessly now: we gazed at each other through eight months of Bach, too awkward to exchange more than a few words.

The Spandau Kantorei that year was a group of twenty high-school age singers charged with performing a cantata in a church in Zehlendorf each Sunday afternoon. The conductor, Hanns-Martin Schneidt, introduced me to the choir more as a colleague than as a barely qualified bass, then launched into a rehearsal which, in a mere two hours, proposed an indelible Bach-image.

First, no hammered beats. He sought the life of the line, his conducting gestures moved *between* the beats. His corrections consisted mainly of shouting the text, then if that failed to produce the necessary marcato or crescendo, shouting it louder. He *assumed* the centrality of the narrative and the theology. He constantly referred to "this piece" as distinct from all other pieces.

This wasn't new to me, but it was especially impressive because the entire two hours explored the German language as sound, and because Schneidt and his singers took for granted a shared religious experience, at one with Bach's material.

"This piece! 161!" Even in rehearsal I began to get its breath, its special temperature. But only when the orchestra joined did I really understand its radical individuality. It is air-music, it has no earthly weight, it is cloud-carried, breeze-blown music expressing the comfort of inevitable death. (Bach writing in Weimar is maybe the last Bach we hear writing completely without any artifice, craftiness, or strategy.)

The Spandau Kantorei sounded great in Cantata 161 in Zehlendorf on a September Sunday in 1960. The choir was young, ardent, and transparent. The orchestra, which includes two flutes, sounded subsumed in flutes. But after the performance, Schneidt was not happy. "I *know* how it should sound. We didn't get there this time. I know The Sound. It was too comfortable! . . . That chorale!" The final movement, where the piece suddenly takes a steep journey through the Passion Chorale into cosmic uncertainty, tracked by a snaking flute obbligato: "The body in the earth will be destroyed by worms, but it will be awakened, transfigured by Christ."

We members of that choir had not enough experience of life to sing such music. Decades later, conducting it in the mid-1970s as part of a funeral for a member of our Emmanuel Music community who had died from AIDS, the piece seemed even more necessary, but still out of reach.

Schneidt casually seemed to assume that every musician knew music as significant as 161. Each week when we came to a cantata I hadn't studied he was completely surprised.

Conducting Bach cantatas was for Schneidt not a cause or a rare books club or in any way a journey into esoterica. It was a need, and also a deed. Studying Bach cantatas was to him a daily, un-sanctimonious religious practice.

A brilliant organist and harpsichordist, in command of the entire literature (rumored to practice "moderately"), Schneidt was, after every performance, bound for a Wursthaus. With a beer in his hand, enough good food, he lapsed into his south German dialect, debriefing and rehashing. I quickly translated a lot of our conversations as advice. The pieces were old honored friends to him. He didn't revere them, he undertook them, he guessed he inevitably fell short of them. He looked forward to the next chance with relish, and a healthy appetite.

Johann Sebastian Bach. Komm du süße Todesstunde; V (2), Coro, orch; BWV 161; BC A 135a: Chorale. Staatsbibliothek Berlin: Mus.ms. Bach P 124.

WHAT DO WE MAKE OF BACH?

SYLVIA KIND

Sylvia Kind played, taught, and lived with a flair that caught
your attention. As her harpsichord student in Berlin in 1960,
I was immediately brought into her fold, her brood. Sylvia's
studio was home base at the Hochschule. The class was studying
Bach toccatas all year; mine were D major and G major. One week
she told me I needed "more candles" in the D major. Or in the C#
minor fugue, Book I, that the upper voice must be "triumphant
and athletic" in its last entrance. Bach, who she always insisted
was a Hungarian, was for her a dramatic composer above all. The
other students learned a lot of Couperin and Rameau, and I was
glad for the little she assigned—amazing Couperin character pieces
which faded to nothing on a piano, the heroic Rameau Gavotte
Varié. But she said, almost every week, "You are a composer, we
must do more Bach."

I bought my first volumes of the new Bach edition in company
with Sylvia, driving across into East Berlin (pre-Wall). We stopped
on the way at her favorite lunch place, Huehner Hugo (the German
Kentucky Fried Chicken), then drove to a music store where she
was well known, and where she encouraged me to stock up: "Poor
music students must have their library any way they can" was her
refrain. Later I worried about further sinking the East German
economy by buying a *St. Matthew* full score for 50 cents.

On the way home we secreted our purchases underneath her
VW in a specially constructed cradle, and she charmed the border
guards, all of whom called her Professor-Doktor and treated her
with the greatest respect as they waved us on with our contraband.

We were, in fact, like baby chickens in her care. A health nut, she often burst into our practice rooms with a chamois bag filled with her "Gesund-Saft," and shouted "Aufmachen!" (open your mouth), squirting the concoction directly into the back of the throat (not choking was the sign of a devoted and experienced student).

In fact, she associated Bach with health. "Bach macht Gesund," she often said when assigning me one of the Preludes and Fugues that was far too hard for me.

Curiosity seekers on the Wannsee would report her break-of-dawn daily skinny dip, another part of her vigorous health regime.

A few years after Berlin she came and stayed with us, and joined us in the Bach *Triple*. In spite of her fine health habits she had a lot of allergies. Our exiled cats hung from the outside kitchen screens, meowing pitifully to be re-admitted. Sylvia was unmoved: "Die Kätze müssen doch warten."

My last abiding memory of Sylvia was knocking on her dressing room door before the *Triple*. "Aufmachen" was heard in a new context, and I discovered Sylvia in her classic warm-up position, a perfect headstand. "Bach macht Gesund."

Johann Sebastian Bach. Tokkaten; cemb; D-Dur; BWV 912. Staatsbibliothek Berlin: Mus.ms. Bach P 286 (13).

FRAU BAUM

*S*oon after arriving in Berlin I found a ground floor apartment on the Waitzstrasse, a pretty tough street in the center of town right off the Kurfürstendamm. (A later visit found the street erased for a freeway.) I would have preferred a better courtyard apartment on the Goethestrasse (I liked being associated with the poet), but the landlady made me nervous when she introduced me to her half-American child by her soldier husband who "resembled" me and had "heartlessly" abandoned her in 1946.

So instead I found Frau Baum, the sort of Isherwood Berlin character I really needed, more than I knew. I asked if my Bach playing, the cello suites on viola, would disturb her. "Go ahead. I hate all music, but Bach I hate less."

I. The G Major, 9 a.m.

Heavy beating on the window by two tough-looking guys, demanding I stop. Ironic, threatening imitation of my sounds and stance. Frau Baum appeared, chased them away, drew me solemnly to the window, fixating on a small apologetic man walking by with a cane and briefcase, with a warning, "Everybody you see on the street is a criminal."

II. The C minor

Even though my window blind is drawn, a cultivated voice from outside: "Every time I hear that piece I remember the day my wife walked out." The next morning, early, Frau Baum with a request: "Play something else, my stool is all hardened up today, Herr Harbison." The C minor – time to move on.

III. The Eb

Frau Baum interrupts my work on one of the most difficult of the suites with a consult: "A Chinese man wants to rent one of the rooms, of course I will not, these people are dirty, as you, Mr. Harbison, of course know." A discussion results, one of our most productive, in which I succeed in convincing her that this attitude is unfair to the applicant, that it will be good for her to be more broadminded.

A week later, success, she gestures to the nice clean clothes the new tenant already has hanging in the single shared bathroom, the many nice friends that come to visit him. Another week later I apply an hour early for the giant metal tuning fork required to heat water for a bath. The bathroom has become an intricate forest of delicate wires all hung with clothes. I remember thinking the rain forest dripping was a little like the opening of Bach Cantata 39.

All too soon the Chinese laundry was terminated. "Herr Harbison, all this trouble you have caused me."

IV. The C major

The simplicity and order of the downward scales are suddenly interrupted by the agonized howls of Frau Baum's adult son, who is hallucinating with a high fever. His lament echoes through the entire flat: "I cannot stay at home. There are twenty men under me, if I am not there they will simply run wild." Frau Baum adds, "My son is simply indispensable, the entire factory upon his shoulders."

V. The D minor

Early in my stay Frau Baum had recommended the Tegernseer, a famous family-style restaurant a block away "full of men who are still ready to fight for the Reich, if we had had more of them

I would never have been raped by the Russians." The Tegernseer was a friendly place, everyone ready to talk, often about the good old days, the late '30s. When I asked what it was about that time, the frequent answer was, "It was more peaceful."

One night I stayed a little too long, getting out just before the locked arms and the unconscious segue into the Horst Wessel Song.

Toward the end of my D minor period, I followed its austere triadic tributaries out to Potsdam to visit the room where Bach improvised, in three voices, the first section of what became the *Musical Offering*. Only a short ride on the S Bahn from the Tegernseer to Frederick the Great's Schloss.

VI. The D major (five-string cello)

Frau Baum enters the room as always, without a knock, is surprised to find me with a visitor, the beautiful exotic Gisela, who has appointed herself girlfriend to all three of the friends— John, Gaston, and John—that she met on a Rhine boat. Pointing to the music on my stand Frau Baum says, rather dismissively, "Bach." Then, pointing to the music on the piano, as if acting as a guide for Gisela, "Herr Harbison's music." I realize I will miss her: she has announced that my new Wirtin, my new landlady, will be Frau Meyer.

Her last advice to me is the rather puzzling admonition to remember that Frau Meyer is very young. In fact, Frau Meyer is in her early thirties, a bit stern, restricts practice and composing hours, and after a month stops by to say: "Herr Gottfried is a very good renter, Herr Wilhelm is a very good renter, Herr Gutbart is a very good renter, but you, Herr Harbison, are not a good renter." A long, severe, seductive stare.

WHAT DO WE MAKE OF BACH?

Arthur Mendel

*A*rthur Mendel was the big Bach scholar in the Princeton Music Department. I knew him then as the editor of the edition of the *St. John Passion* we studied, and as the tough mentor of many of the music history graduate students, to whom he farmed out volumes of the New Bach Edition to prepare for publication. Some of my friends showed me their work—microfilms of parts and scores, cantatas I met later, actually *sounding* as we performed them at Emmanuel Church.

It was a little hard to imagine that Mendel had entered the university late, after a career as a conductor. He and his students seemed locked into the few details they had discovered as divergent from the old Bach Gesellschaft Edition. One of the young editors seemed surprised when I remarked on the unusual sonority he was editing, as if the sonic dimension seldom intruded in his workplace. Many of Mendel's grad students were discouraged from performing, which he regarded as an activity inferior to their scholarship.

Quite soon after arriving at Princeton University Graduate School some of us mounted a performance of Bach Cantata 4, in which I volunteered to play continuo harpsichord. I was not bothered (but should have been) by my inexperience. I just assumed it was like playing jazz—use your ear, play something close to the chords you perceive to be going past.

Wrong.

I played a lot of clinkers. Unfortunately, Arthur Mendel was in the audience. After offering his general support for the project, he addressed the continuo issue: "Your playing was imaginative! In the wrong way. This music is one *specific* harmony after another."

Abashed, humiliated, I did know that about Bach's harmony. Since then I have constantly reconfirmed that continuo keyboard never gets easy. Most pieces require a predictive route, mapped in advance. It is like being an orchestral harpist—sight-reading is foolhardy.

Immediately upon hearing Mendel's critique, I recalled a roughly similar experience from seven years earlier. Shouldn't I have remembered it as I launched myself as a continuo player?

The Nassau Jazz Band, a good cottage Dixieland band that I often played with along with my friend Tom Artin, was playing Princeton Reunions in early summer of my sophomore year in high school. On a Saturday morning I got a call from someone looking for the kid who played piano in that Princeton band, which was, at that that moment, me. They needed a replacement for Dick Wellstood, who had become "unavailable" for the afternoon. The group in question was led by the great Basie trumpeter Buck Clayton, and included trombonist Vic Dickinson and the bassist-photographer Milt Hinton.

I showed up, raw and excited. I knew, worshipped, their playing, knew all the tunes, imagined myself an experienced and original player. I was, at 15, entranced with the intricacies of jazz harmony, a young master of substitutions, alterations, surprise deviations. When I played piano duets at home entertainments with my uncle, the Very Very Reverend Erdman Harris (a very solid, expert '20s piano player as I would later understand), I was bored with his devotion to standard (Urtext) harmony.

It was somewhere in the third tune that I noticed Buck Clayton eyeing me during his solo—I was convinced I was gassing them with my kaleidoscopic inventions (they seemed, all of them, friendly and appreciative). But at the end of "You Took Advantage of Me," Buck came back to talk. "Hey kid, great chords behind my solo!" (pause) "Trouble is, they ain't in the tune." A stern look from Buck, almost fatherly, as if to say, "If you're a smart kid you'll remember this."

Buck wasn't implying that jazz was not the free, improvisational palace of art I believed it to be. He was saying its magic is collaborative, disciplined, and ignited by rigorous listening.

And keyboard continuo? Geometric, framed, jacketed improvisation.

Richard Rodgers & Lorenz Hart. "You took advantage of me." *The Real Book*. Milwaukee, WI: Hal Leonard.

WHAT DO WE MAKE OF BACH?

WILLIAM H. SCHEIDE

*N*ear the end of my two years as a graduate student at Princeton, I was enflamed with the idea of putting on a big Bach cantata concert. Somehow some money was found for soloists and players (I later found out who one backer had been).

Tom Hilbish offered his marvelous Princeton High School choir. I had met some good singers when I sang in his chorus for Sal Martirano's *Shakespearian Rag*: the fiery tenor Clarence Moore had a fist fight with that composer when leaving a rehearsal a little early, so I knew he had enough temperament for the tenor aria in Cantata 97. I considered that aria the crux of our concert for two reasons: 1) I believed it to be the finest of Bach's violin arias, and 2) it was to be played by a marvelous player, Rose Mary Pedersen, with whom I had fallen in love.

How much of this project might come back to that last condition?

I enjoy all the perhapses that have come to surround this aria. That perhaps its comprehensive technical demands, so like those required in the six solo violin pieces, indicate the availability of a certain player, who was perhaps Johann Pisendel, who was perhaps again in Leipzig for this, one of the later cantatas. [Pisendel's inept use of quotes from Bach's solo violin pieces in a concerto of his own indicates how highly he valued those pieces he perhaps premiered.]

When Rose Mary Harbison and I had a second chance to do Cantata 97 together, at Emmanuel Church, fifty years to the day after the first one, I was able to confirm (nourished by a half-century of devoted Bach cantata study) the sovereignty of the piece's violin aria—able to perceive subtleties in its disguised ground-bass construction, in its flood of melodic invention, that necessarily eluded me in 1963.

Cantata 97 is a perfect concert cantata: four soloists, arias for all, wide distribution of instrumental responsibilities, a rather neutral text, more a suite than a cantata. It is so non-committal, textually, that I felt it was essential to counter it on our program with a more devotional, narrative piece, Cantata 72.

The tenor aria begins and ends with a complete Sinfonia for violin and continuo. Then the singer and player share the melody's abundant, varied ideas, sometimes simplifying, sometimes elaborating. The text placidly expresses trust in God's grace. In spite of this, the music urgently builds to the statement *"Nichts wird mich verletzen"* ("Nothing will harm me"). The repeated *nichts* is dramatically declaimed by the tenor and violinist. As we came to that place, a commotion in the audience—shouts of *nichts*, nearly synchronized with ours, then a clatter, as the shouter—William Scheide, who had stood to help galvanize the moment—fell back noisily into his chair.

Of course he knew the piece, William Scheide, inheritor of an oil fortune, Princeton resident and philanthropist, founder in the late 1940s of the Bach Aria Group, which was the first proselytizer for the cantata literature in the United States. When I was around twelve years old, already what is known as a Bach-hound, I was invited to Scheide's house to hear his Baroque organ (which seemed to occupy about half the house) and see one of the two Bach portraits in existence: the famous Hausman portrait. Its owner was proud to display it, to discuss whether it was the first of the two or the painter's copy, to talk about the painter's visit to Leipzig, where he asked to paint the town's most distinguished musicians and was directed to Bach and Bach's trumpet player (Johann Gottfried Reiche, depicted holding a part from a never-found Bach cantata, a piece he may have been playing when he died of a heart attack soon after the portraits were completed). I loved hearing these stories, and I loved hearing Scheide navigate one of J.S. Bach's chorale preludes on his organ, which even at modest volume seemed amazingly loud in the small living room.

William Scheide was a friend of my parents, a fixture at concerts in our town and, as I later learned, an important Bach scholar. Connections between Bach cantatas of the second Leipzig year and cantatas by Bach's uncle Ludwig were the subject of one of his important essays. He also played a benevolent role in my life, sponsoring performances as conductor and composer. He was, at least according to a hint from Thomas Hilbish, the main sponsor of the Princeton Bach concert. The recording of that concert served as my audition (along with various mainly new-music conducting jobs in Boston) for the Music Directorship of the Cantata Singers. My work with that group, more than my reputation as a composer, was crucial to my perilous tenure case at MIT. My teaching at MIT gave me a place to hide for many years, finding a community, writing pieces, becoming a composer.

As I write this William Scheide is one hundred years old. For years his Christmas card was a page from the manuscript of Cantata 33, which he owns, a facsimile of which he generously underwrote a few years ago.

He remains to me a beacon of enlightened life in music. He believed that Bach's cantatas could be appreciated by a wide audience. This has never really happened, but his method—engaging well-known performers who could bring their listeners to the music—made sense in the forties and still does.

I will never forget my first hearing of "Gott versorget," the grand soprano aria from 187, with Eileen Farrell and Robert Bloom. And I will surely never forget the 97 tenor aria in the cantorial voice of Jan Peerce, with the elegant Viennese accented violin of Isadore Cohen. Was it not, perhaps, as *authentic*, as communicative of the music's truth as any performance since?

Johann Sebastian Bach. In allen meinen Taten; V (4), Coro, orch; BWV 97; BC A 189. No. 4 Ich traue seiner Gnaden, Violino I. Staatsbibliothek Berlin: Mus.ms. Bach St 64.

ROSE MARY PEDERSEN

*T*hroughout my Bach-saturated year in Berlin (1960-61), through the good offices of my harpsichord teacher Sylvia Kind, I rehearsed and eventually performed two sonatas. My partner for the monumental *Flute Sonata in E minor* was Renée Clivio Walz (whose name and temperament summarized the complicated Swiss cultural mix). In the B minor violin sonata I worked with Takaya Urakawa, a fine musician who offered, with delicate diplomacy, both musical suggestions and hints about the differences between American and Japanese social expectations. These were acts of friendship. Rather than be offended by behavior of mine I deemed routine and he thought boorish, he explained differences, with great patience, thus protecting our time together.

It was Takaya, drawing on his reputation with our fellow students, who organized my only performance of the year, at the Haus am Wannsee.

A year later, in Princeton, it was the B minor sonata that was the focus of my first duo rehearsal with Rose Mary Pedersen, a young woman I already knew interested me very much, with whom I had worked in a variety of ensembles but with whom I had never, until then, heard in chamber music.

We borrowed a room (where was it?), with a harpsichord, (whose?), and with few words exchanged began the sonata. The long F#, the long E, each flowering for a moment into a simple five-note connection, then the shining double stops extending the phrase. As this unfolded—recognition, confirmation, accord, consternation. Above all, the marking of a common center. She had told me Bach was her favorite composer, her home site, but this can mean a lot of things. By the end of the first movement I knew that in her case this was not just a devotion to the spirit and generosity of this music, but a trust in it, a willingness to let it speak.

What I heard, at the same time in that reading of the Bach B minor first movement, is the loneliness that often inhabits the undertone of a great master's work, the habitation of a realm so rarely visited, with so little company. To find that secret in a piece of music, the performer needs an inner life, a kind of solitary experience that, I later learned, was part of Rose Mary Pedersen's makeup.

I sensed a person for whom art costs too much, for whom the sharing of that intense experience with others is often painful and risky.

I knew what that might be like.

I sensed joy, possibility, danger, complication, inextricability. A fulcrum, a magnet, a talisman.

We began the second movement.

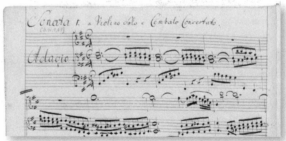

Johann Sebastian Bach. Sonaten; vl, cemb; h-Moll; BWV 1014. I Adagio.
Staatsbibliothek Berlin: Mus.ms. Bach P 229.

ROBERT D. LEVIN

*D*uring my Junior Fellowship years at Harvard I began hearing about a remarkable undergraduate, Robert Levin, who was making completions of Mozart pieces. He was about to present two of them on the final concert of his senior year, a *Double Concerto for Violin, Piano and Orchestra* (in which Rose Mary Harbison and I were invited to participate as soloist and conductor), and a string quintet movement. The intermediary in bringing us together was the violinist in our string quartet, Bentley Layton (now a distinguished professor in the department of Religious Studies at Yale). I was especially intrigued by Levin's project, having had my own attempts at completing Mozart torsos rejected by the Harvard Music Department a few years before.

I knew Levin's resonant bass voice as an omniscient DJ on Harvard radio, but nothing could prepare me for the first meeting, an encounter with someone uniquely, completely immersed and versed in music, from every standpoint—composition, performance, scholarship. This was evident in the fast-paced, wide-ranging three-hour encounter in which began a conversation that continues fifty years later.

There was nothing off-putting or show-off about the assurance that animated the young man's talk: it was simply a fact, a force. About twenty minutes in, I will never forget, the discussion paused on Bach Cantata 27, some detail in the opening chorus. Levin went to the piano and proceeded to play the entire chorus—pacings and dispositions all accurate, narrating a couple of points about it as he played. I perceived that he was ready to do that with a large part of the musical literature.

Oddly enough, though our ostensible subject was our Mozart collaboration, Bach cantatas held the center that day, both of us recognizing a rare chance to talk about a repertoire we had both been exploring actively for many years. There were few recordings available; much of the music had to be learned from the scores, which was part of the fun. We talked about Bob's first exposure to the pieces with Nadia Boulanger, and mine through the very different agency of the Bach Aria Group.

I had by then conducted no more than six or seven of the cantatas in college and graduate school, and had studied about that many more. I was not reluctant to tap Bob's greater expertise, especially in 1968, when I was appointed conductor of the Cantata Singers and Ensemble. Not even owning the scores, I felt I needed to devote July 1969 to study. Each day I drove from Token Creek to the University of Wisconsin library and spent the day reading one volume of the Bach Gesellschaft. Twenty-plus days later I started back over the ones I wanted to see again. Often in the evenings I called Bob, rightly assuming he would probably know any cantata that came up. He made suggestions, of pieces to go back to, or watch out for.

Obviously the forty minutes or so was barely an introduction to each piece. But I believe I got the message quite often, the particular sound and character of the individual movements, the immense unpredictable variety of the entire opus. Certain pieces jumped off the page, never to be pinned there again. Others I frankly missed, pieces I later discovered to be too strange and subtle to be grasped quickly, including some eventual favorites.

(I did a program of these great oddballs in my third year with Cantata Singers: 109, 48, 44.)

Our initial performance collaboration, Mozart's Concerto in C major, K. 503 and the completion of the Mozart Double Concerto, was my first encounter with Bob as improviser, fashioning distinct cadenzas for the K.503 in every rehearsal. He asked me to write a cadenza for the Double, which I did, a forest of early sixties counter-rhythmic complexity. As our friendship continued, we continued to divide our time between composing, improvising, and research (I suspect him of being a secret crackerjack swing-era virtuoso).

One of his skills, continuo playing, is rarely heard in recent years. When I got a chance to record, with Cantata Singers, two of the cantatas in first (!) recordings, I invited Bob to play the organ, unwittingly committing ourselves to through-takes on most of the movements. Bob's restless, inventive mind led him to re-realize the continuo part each time through each piece, making splices seldom possible. Each version, with new chord spacings and melodic ideas, was equally plausible, a textbook lesson in a skill scarce in our time. But try mapping one into another!

Robert Levin is famous as a Mozart performer, scholar, and restorer. I think of his taking forward promising Mozart incipits as a kind of restoration to the repertoire of pieces Wolfgang Amadeus Mozart lacked time to finish. His habitation of Mozart's language is the fruit of a lifetime of study with both ear and mind. But his command of Bach language, as evident in his many recordings of keyboard pieces, but especially in his lordly continuo skills, speaks of an equal, very uncommon access to the world of the most comprehensive of composers.

Much has been made of how much Bob Levin is like Mozart—
the improvisatory gifts, the natural technical fluency, the theatrical
entertainer stage personality. He even looks a little like Mozart.

But in one particular way he is more like Bach. For Levin,
the structural detail, the analytic route, is one with the expressive
hierarchy. Understanding resolves into communication. This is
a Bachian secret: that what moves us is more perfect language,
a higher syntax.

Johann Sebastian Bach. Wer weiß wie nahe mir mein Ende; V (4), Coro, orch;
BWV 27; BC A 138; BWV Anh. III 170. 1 [Choral & Recitativo]: Wer weiß, wie
nahe mir mein Ende. Staatsbibliothek Berlin: Mus.ms. Bach P 164.

CRAIG SMITH

*O*ne afternoon in 1969, in a break during a rehearsal for Cantata 95, the soprano Jane Bryden remembered something she'd been meaning to tell me: "I rehearse a lot right across this street at Craig Smith's place. You should meet him. He knows every Schubert song."

While guessing this might be an exaggeration, I very soon found myself in the presence of a twenty-one year old Schubert—round body, round eyeglasses, rumpled clothes, endless curiosity. He greeted me (greeted everyone) with a unique mix of formal courtesy and friendly enthusiasm. It soon became clear that Craig Smith had, in fact, studied every Schubert song.

Craig arrived in Boston at 20, both countrified and supremely well educated. He often recalled his first night in Boston, at the Y: "I opened the men's room door to a daisy chain that would have made the Etruscans blush." Lewiston, Idaho and Washington State University in Spokane collaborated with Craig's ravenous musical appetite to implant splendid fundamentals.

Gunther Schuller's New England Conservatory in the late '60s, its Golden Age, offered true visionaries: Rudolf Kolisch, Russell Sherman, and John Heiss. Craig was able to drink it in: knowledge, eccentricity, extreme commitment—eventually his own essential virtues. Craig's respect for his teachers was one of his abiding qualities. This applied to his Lewiston teachers as well as the two he referred to through his life as Mr. Sherman and Mr. Kolisch.

When I met Craig he aspired to be a Lieder pianist, partnering and guiding singers through a literature that already inhabited him. It was mainly his bond with young singers that brought him to my concerts with Boston's Cantata Singers. Craig knew a lot of the Bach keyboard music, but his familiarity with the cantatas was sketchy. The music caught fire in his imagination. Discovering that we were both nocturnals, there were midnight phone calls. 127! 10! 20!!

Craig was at the same time a tenor in the Emmanuel Church Choir. The director was a distinguished but troubled, alcoholic harpsichordist well-known in the community who one day became too helpless to continue. Could anyone conduct the rest of the rehearsal? Craig had never conducted anything. Never opportunistic or aggressive by temperament, Craig nevertheless often found himself in the right place at the right time. He stepped in, relinquishing the post only with his death forty years later.

Craig immediately began to redesign the program and the position after two weeks, convincing Al Kershaw, Emmanuel's jazz-expert pastor, to let him lead Bach cantatas in the service. At twenty-one, first with volunteers, then incrementally with professionals, Craig started the Emmanuel Bach Cantata Cycle. Within a few years he and I were reversing roles: he was teaching me about Bach.

Rose Mary Harbison and I played in the first cantatas Craig conducted at Emmanuel. The mysterious effectiveness of his conducting revealed itself promptly! He appeared to do little. But the performers did well. It was not that he lacked ideas about the music. Ideas were transmitted through his absorption in the music. You saw little, but that little opened all the right channels.

In the early days he often asked me for recommendations of cantatas of special interest (though we both later concluded that all of them were somehow in that category). I remember mentioning 165, one of Bach's precious Seraphic Weimar cantatas. This time I was a listener, not a performer. A round heavy man standing in front of a lot of performers I knew, gestures unspecific, but enabling, encouraging, releasing. And the Craig Smith trademark: a perfect sense of tempo.

The composer Edward Cohen remarked that he never heard Craig set a wrong tempo. They changed from year to year, but they were physical, calculated, suited to the occasion. He had a rare conductor-gift of setting a pulse unambiguously, clear to everyone, and holding it, in an elastic frame. No sag, no tinkering.

Craig was a grandiose planner. He would imagine extraordinary projects, many of them stretching over years, expressing his favorite theory: to know a composer you needed to know every note (with Bach, Schubert, Handel and Schütz he was at least very close to it). Magical programs, sequences, the right pieces, people, places. He would howl in indignation as the practical problems—money, space, personnel—were raised by colleagues, boards, friends. Then, often, something like the thing he had described was conjured up.

There was a catch, however, one to understand if you were to remain a friend of Craig. He described all his schemes as if they were definitely on. They were, in his mind! But if you didn't know to write it in pencil, you could find yourself at odds with him, disappointed, confused.

"Let's perform the *Art of the Fugue* with twelve pianists, straight through, no intermission, a benefit for Emmanuel Music—everyone will want to do it." One of Craig's last and best ideas. By then most of us knew to cross our fingers. But twelve pianists agreed to play, and only one, Craig, dropped out. His strength and eyesight failing, he was heard often working on the first phrase in Fugue I, trailing off, but returning with a marvelous insight into what separated these pieces from all other Bach fugues: "They are keyboard fugues, but they follow the fingers least."

The *Art of the Fugue* played through without a pause for a full house by an amazing train of opinionated, devoted pianists, Craig accepting the community's gratitude, dressed that night like a casino impresario greeting his gamblers—there could not have been a more just, final, public event for his reign at Emmanuel.

When Craig decided to do the complete cycle of Bach cantatas he had only been leading the Emmanuel Choir for a few weeks. In the '70s, many of the pieces were available only in poor materials, or not at all. Most of the players and singers had no experience with the music. I remember late night calls, Craig pasting up parts from a cut-up score, rehearsal seven hours away, two volunteer players having dropped out, suddenly asking, "John, what are you writing right now?" "It is an opera, a Shakespeare opera." "Too big, too big, no one should be writing anything larger than a trio." "Craig, who dropped out this time?"

Eventually stalwart regulars emerged, who hated to miss a cantata, with their long hair and their hippie outfits, a vagabond harmonious circle, stability marred only by growing dialectic tension in the Early Music world. This tension both rankled and intrigued. Certainly there was a lot to learn from this movement. But the air of superiority, of ultimate authority, the mannered theatrical exaggerated assertion of correctness?

We resisted, and absorbed it. And gradually achieved concord, if not conversion.

Much was lost to the Bach cantata world when Craig died at 60. We hear some of it on his recordings. We hear one of the few who conducted them all. The more encounters a conductor has, the less generalized and formulaic he must be. Each piece raises questions you haven't heard before.

There is something unusual in the sonority of his performances. This is related to the speed, attack, and balance, but it is best described as a now-unfashionable weightiness. Once, coming in for Sunday after Craig became ill overnight, I offered the downbeat of Cantata 197 and simply took the Ride, the sound as Craig rehearsed it. I remember thinking, "How does he get this?," and thinking it was a combination of his physical presence, serious intent, and the blunt quality of the gesture. Lightness and crisp articulation solve many problems. But many of the pieces have a gravity and density that needs to be represented by a sense of bulk, space, importance.

The first recorded Bach conductors—Mengelberg, Klemperer, Scherchen—all knew how to find it. They are all out of date now; so is Craig. Yet I sense that the future of Bach performance leads to more variety of sound, a more philosophic, theological interpretation that requires timbral imagination.

Around 2004 Craig suddenly became reluctant to cede a week of his job to another conductor. At first I missed the point, but it soon was clear that he had begun to find he was running out of time.

His final visits to the pieces that had formed the center of his musical life, and his communal life, were a revelation. Rather than display discoveries, insights, ideas, he seemed more than ever reluctant to disturb them. He wished instead to let them breathe, let the players and singers find their voice in them.

The Emmanuel community which assembled to help in his care still felt both guided and set free by his leadership. My last evening with him, such a vigorous conversation that I was again convinced his death was far off, involved excited discussion about pieces we had both known for thirty years. Also, a program he had dreamed up to frame a new piece I had written and had just shown him.

On his piano the day after he died, Cantata 73, the piece scheduled for the weekend, amid a sort of spontaneous wake at his apartment both natural and eerie. In his last days he must have been trying to travel the route of that cantata. The same words at the beginning and at the end: "Lord as you will it," first hectoring, angry, desperate, then after a vision of descending wings, stoic, brave, resolved. [But with a final chorale appended that sounds like a shout of protest.]

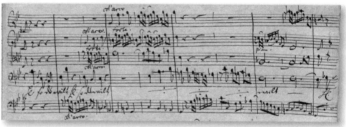

Johann Sebastian Bach. Herr wie du willt so schicks mit mir; V (3), Coro, orch; BWV 73; BC A 35. 4. Aria (B): Herr, so du willt. Staatsbibliothek Berlin: Mus.ms. Bach P 664.

FRED GOLDSTEIN

*N*one of us knew any businessmen. The Emmanuel Music community in the early years appeared to be ragamuffin hippies, with no idea of how commerce worked, no concept of marketing or promotion. Into that scene walked the Vice President of the Advent Corporation, Fred Goldstein.

In the late '60s, early 70's, Advent Corporation was a beacon presence in the hi-fi industry. Their corporate image was free and loose. I remember a walk-in-and-find-Fred-anytime policy, and we did, amid a sea of disheveled desks and casual-looking, gregarious employees.

Fred Goldstein was breezy, confident, raffish, on-the-move. I recall that before he turned up as a cellist in the cantata orchestra some of us had played a lot of chamber music with him. Fred played with uncanny anticipation of each event, and an un-fastidious attitude. He had studied the basic chamber music literature with Leo Kauter (whose music we also read together), and it was clear that this training led Fred to regard chamber music as a form of celebration.

The Bach cantatas were great pieces Fred did not know (unlike the Haydn Quartets). He received them with joy, and didn't stop there. He quickly put Advent Corporation's resources behind publicizing and supporting our events. "Bring Back Bach Alive" posters began appearing all over town. Listener numbers increased at the Sunday services and evening concerts. The yearly Mozart Birthday Concert sold out every free seat. Goldstein's years at Emmanuel coincided with what is now called Outreach.

Fred's advocacy extended to the parallel Bach cantata-centered organization, The Cantata Singers, of which I was the conductor. The Advent recordings of Cantatas 7, 44, and 101 preserve a moment in time in the history of Boston music-making. Making the first ever recording of one of the most significant of all the cantatas, BWV 101, remains one of the most precious, irreplaceable moments in the musical life of all who participated.

Fred Goldstein drove a Cadillac, showed up in his corporate office on his own hours, sent the wine back, spent money and time with unrepentant generosity. All of that was heard in the bass lines he supplied us for many years.

LP record jacket: *Johann Sebastian Bach: Cantatas 7, 44 and 101*. The Cantata Singers & Ensemble; John Harbison, conductor. Advent Corporation [RD-1015]: 1973.

DAVID SATZ

*D*avid Satz, because he is a clarinet player, was not a participant in Emmanuel Music's cantata performances, except in the radical re-orchestrations by Craig Smith that graced some of his collaborations with the stage director Peter Sellars. Nevertheless, David played a central role. He was a very searching musician, whose main musical studies were with the great chamber music violinist Rudolf Kolisch. For many years, Satz was Emmanuel's recording engineer, and an important benefactor.

The last was a strange chapter. Upon receiving a significant bequest from his industrialist father, Satz embarked on a concentrated campaign to spend it down to nothing as fast as possible. The beneficiaries were Emmanuel Music's Bach Cantata program, and the radical political activities of the Weather Underground. I guess it is possible to say that both organizations experienced very productive periods.

But it is David as engineer that I must recall here. At one point his always very alert recordings seemed to take on a special luster. I was at his house when I heard his splendid pickup of Bach Cantata BWV 163, to that point the most fortunate of all the fifty or so performances I had conducted at Emmanuel. He revealed that he had embraced a new technology to produce this remarkable sound: a crackpot inventor friend had introduced a kind of attachment called the SNERD, a new patented formula, a kind of finishing loop. The material is recorded in a counter-intuitive way—damping out highs and articulation—and then the SNERD is applied, and presto: revelations!

Unfortunately, I neglected then to get a copy of BWV 163 and a number of other cantatas, so I was stunned when applying for such at his house (as he was interrupted by calls from his many girlfriends, always answered by, "I know, I haven't called"), he announced that the SNERD formula was lost, and with it the last three years of recordings that used the method.

Twenty years later, the inventor of the SNERD suddenly remembered the code, and copies of the missing Cantatas appeared in my mailbox. Were the performances, were the recordings as perfect as I remembered?

LORRAINE HUNT LIEBERSON

*M*y first real conversation with the young violist Lorrie Hunt took place after a Sunday afternoon Pro Arte Chamber Orchestra performance of my *Elegiac Songs*, led by David Hoose. The conductor invited a few of us to go out to supper, and I remember thinking what a bright addition to the scene this recently arrived player would be—not an intellectual, but someone fired by music (it confirmed my long-standing partiality to viola players as company). A few weeks later we together formed the divided viola section in Cantata 4 at Emmanuel.

(I had first encountered Lorraine's name on a recording by the Berkeley Chamber Players of Dallapiccola's *Quattro Esercisi*, a piece I was preparing to play in Purchase in 1965.)

Young Lorrie Hunt—a fine violist, excellent sound and skills, well-prepared, musical.

I was as startled as anyone when she stepped forward as the emergency substitute Eve, out of the orchestra, in part III of Haydn's *Creation*. That brilliant, Germanic, silver soprano sound, a thrill in its almost too-present intensity, indelible. I conducted a lot of Bach with her at Emmanuel in her soprano days. The seraphic aria in 127, *Die Seele ruht*, was not really right for her. It came at the time of her kooky Elvira with Smith and Sellars, also not really right. But I have never heard the 127 pieces sung with such soulful soaring rapture. It remains one of the treasures among my private recordings.

As she transitioned downward, many of the Bach pieces, like the Cantata 33 aria, suited her perfectly and were delivered with a very specific sense of the text, the occasion, her relationship to the collaborating instruments.

During her time at Emmanuel, Lorraine was the consummate ensemble singer. She participated in all the choir's performances, as well as their early recordings of Bach, Schütz, and my motets. Her favorite piece of music, she often said, was Schütz's Psalm 116, a magnificent 16-minute choral piece.

As she became somewhat belatedly well-known, her work habits never changed. Her vocal practice was rigorously detailed, the refining of every issue from the smallest motive to the biggest phrase. I heard her practicing that way only a few times, with amazement at her patience. Her absolute precision of pitch and rhythm was the first order of business, along with any background pertaining to the piece that she could find. "Interpretation" was not a self-conscious element—it was released, discovered when the most mundane elements were in place.

Working with Lorraine, I often thought of Bach's statement, "Anyone can compose as well as I do if they will work as hard." Lorraine's secret was the work. Of course she had fire, talent, drive, and independence. But in every generation some have those. Lorraine re-set the work standard.

And she made her own decisions, always—in spite of managers, presenters, and handlers—about what she would sing.

Often when giving some sort of seminar about Bach for a group of singers, I was asked questions about Lorraine. The questions were often framed in terms of charisma, or magic. But over the years, hearing many singers begin with vocal gift or temperament or ambition quite comparable to hers, I know that her difference was her insistence on being a total, fundamental musician. It's what allowed her to get better and better, to surpass herself because she kept the foundation so solid, able to support and release that expressive viola voice.

Then comes an interesting question: What was Lorraine Hunt Lieberson really like? Here, I am speculating, because in my experience she seemed two people in one body. There was a philosophic, thoughtful, often melancholic resonance in her singing, an opening up of meanings and possibilities, actually beyond explanation.

There was Lorraine, who often ran the phone message machine out twice in a row in a delightful stream-of-consciousness hardly philosophic. Lorraine, the California girl with the irresistible throaty laugh, who seemed to have left all the conflict and turmoil behind, on stage. There was Lorraine who swam with the dolphins, who chose the seat in the sun at the café.

The Lorraine as much missed, by those lucky enough to know her, as the glorious presence on stage.

Perhaps only Peter Lieberson, whose Muse she was, who wrote for her with such complete insight, really ever knew enough to fit all this together.

Both of these Lorraines had to withdraw even further into privacy and discipline during her illness. But it is important to remember the roles privacy and discipline *always* played in making her the artist she was. When such a person leaves us far too soon it is possible to freight all their work with the presence of the early death, and "hear" it through that filter. But if Lorraine Hunt Lieberson had lived to 80, her performances, early and late, would move us as surely they do now. They derive their substance from her answer to the calling of the artist: work, truth, generosity.

ESSAYS

Joh. Seb. Bach

BACH OR JESUS?
EMMANUEL'S TIME OF TROUBLE

*H*ow to tell this story. The conflict was so ancient, so full of timeless questions. Here's Richard Dyer, *The Boston Globe* music critic, summarizing:

The arts are a powerful but dangerous ally to religion. They can carry the message, they can also run away with it. Music can convey emotion, faith, wonder, doubt and questions, as least as powerfully as words can; it is not particularly suitable to the exposition of doctrine and dogma.

1992: A new Rector, Michael Kuhn, with the support of the Episcopal Diocese, was intent on making Emmanuel a real Episcopal Church. The congregation, in the contentious spirit of the previous Rector, Al Kershaw, defined the independence of its thought and its mission. Some of the challenges uttered at that time by opponents of the church's arts ministry:

Al Kershaw erred in giving non-believers (i.e. choir members as Vestry members) positions of authority.

Emmanuel was taken over by greedy, power-hungry musicians who would do anything to save their jobs.

Emmanuel Music has claimed J.S. Bach as its savior, while some of us prefer Jesus Christ.

The Bach cantata texts are bad for our self-image—paternal, stern, and depressing.

Bach's music is sucking up the Glory that ought to go to God.

Two years of strife, without resolution. For better or worse it pitted the music program and Craig Smith against Michael Kuhn. The Vestry voted to remove the Rector, who refused to leave. The resolution was consigned to Canon 21, eventually there was a trial, with testimony on both sides.

Surprisingly, the Rector was removed, and assigned to a parish in New Orleans. Further conclusions appeared in Bishop Johnson's Godly Judgment: the church reduced to mission status, Music Director Craig Smith to expect termination for "financial reasons." Later the Bishop, heretofore impatient with Emmanuel's renegade temperament, suddenly made an inspired appointment: William Wallace, a Lutheran pastor then serving in an AIDS ministry, as interim priest.

The final chapter. Bishop Johnson, a former General in the Strategic Air Command, was found responsible for unacceptable conduct involving female parishioners and committed suicide.

Twenty-five years later. A strong spiritual-artistic bond now exists between Emmanuel Church and its current Rector Pam Werntz and Emmanuel Music's Artistic Director Ryan Turner and Executive Director Pat Krol. The cantatas continue, the church is still or again a unique community force. But it still seems necessary, every week, to establish as clearly as possible why we do what we do there.

At my testimony for the Canon 21 Proceedings I included the following:

> Many in today's world seek the world of the spirit, but are searching for the door. It may not be the Bible-reading or the sermon. Emmanuel Music enlists the help of two great Evangelists, Bach and Schütz, who may, for some, provide an opening, a way through.

It is not an end-point, there is no end-point. It is the possibility of finding more than we thought we needed. The sounds have the power to open our hearts. At Emmanuel we are paid, but we play for a lot more than money. We play for listeners, we play for ourselves, for high stakes. We play this music often enough and well enough to discover, in community, that it takes us to a place we could not have described or known, which has in these and old times been called faith, religion, belief, enlightenment.

BACH IN MISSISSIPPI

*O*ur friend John Mudd had come up with an unusual idea of how a group of us might go to Jackson, Mississippi for the summer of 1964—to replace the faculty of Tougaloo College.

That faculty needed relief. They were teaching at a liberal black college in a city that was already becoming tense, anticipating what their citizens called "invasion" from the north. Tougaloo, during that winter, had been designated the headquarters of "The Movement" during Freedom Summer. It was easy to guess that the next months in Mississippi would be consequential, and we wanted to be there. On the way down, we heard that three Freedom Summer activists—Andrew Goodman, Mickey Schwerner, both white, and James Chaney, black—had been lynched.

We began teaching the day after we arrived. The heat hit like a heavy breath as we got off the plane. We knew that the best time for classes was before 9 a.m.. My first teaching job; I wanted it to go well. Ate a Mississippi breakfast—grits, greens and chitlins—at 7 a.m., met the class in second-year harmony, gave a little ear test. Promising. Switched to potato fritters, stayed with ear training for a few weeks. Then one day a student said: "Show us chords."

In all my early harmony training we had begun with Bach. I didn't know yet what a hard place to start it was. I played a chorale: "Show us *those* chords." Before long, I was trying to teach similar progressions at the piano. I-IV-V, V-IV-I.

I showed them how we, Bach and the concert composers, do it. "Sounds wrong." I played it again, bringing out the pleasure of voices moving in opposite directions. "Still doesn't sound right." I asked them to play it the way they wanted it. They did. They played it the way I would play it in a blues band.

"But in this music, we do it differently." What was I really saying to them? It was the first of many language difficulties to be worked on all summer.

Outside of class, other complications. The third day, in our cart at the supermarket, we found a scrawled note: "Nigger-lover. Go Home." A few days later, returning to campus, we were ordered by FBI agents, guns drawn, to open our instrument cases. King, Abernathy, Jackson, the whole leadership was on campus for a "secure" meeting.

Gunshots from trucks with mounted artillery caused us to move away from the lead-reinforced wall nearest the road. No tuner or piano mover was willing to come on campus. Rosie had learned to tune before coming, having guessed at the problem, brought lots of tuning equipment. The basketball team moved the piano, still in their shorts, like a giant centipede carrying a coffin. They left it, legs off, flat to the floor, we fetched a large spatula.

Later, a serious inflammatory mistake. We drove to Jackson with one of our students, the tenor Walter Turnbull in the front seat. Parked in the lot, went in to a store. Came out, got into the car, suddenly surrounded by fifteen guys with tire irons. Drove through them fast, then guessed (!) which way the street ran. A wrong guess meant the Jackson police, where an ambivalent FBI would not protect us.

The trip to town was in search of music for Walter Turnbull

to sing on our concerts. We settled instead on something we brought, the tenor aria from Bach Cantata 101. Walter had been well-taught by Professor Ariel Lovelace, a proud distinguished man who couldn't see why northern grad students were needed at Tougaloo. It was not easy for Walter to get a grip on the angular music of BWV 101. He said it was so strange, it filled him with fear.

A week before, as we left our rehearsal, Walter bravely fended off a family of rattlesnakes who had attacked us on the chapel steps. But the Bach, far from his world at that time, was not reflex, not instinct. Later, as conductor of the Harlem Boychoir, Walter led his choir in the spirituals and hymns of his youth, he led them also in Bach. The experience between us and gifted Tougaloo students like Walter played out later as both enrichment and discomfort.

What were we doing in Mississippi? Certainly we were disrupting, very deliberately. Our group of young enthusiastic teachers taught what interested us, at our accustomed level of discourse. The probably mostly astonished students heard lectures on Yeats and Eliot, Emerson and Thoreau, concerts of music by Brahms and Schoenberg. What were we thinking? Was it arrogance or heedlessness? A few students gratefully followed us north. Most, in this phase of the Civil Rights Movement, didn't question the minute presence of African-Americans among our faculty, or in our subject matter. We were constantly and unjustifiably surprised by their yearning for the house in the suburbs, two-car garage, comfortable job image of white America. Their prim, dressy in-class outfits made a strange contrast with our scruffy on-to-the-future radical threads.

It was our rough presence in Mississippi that had the main effect. It was very seriously disrupting. It said above all that the powerless in their culture had supporters, that the country and the world were watching, that change was inevitable. Within a year or two Jackson was more functionally integrated than the northern cities from which we came.

When I looked at the faces of the young men with brickbats who would seem to want to kill us I saw—outrage. How could we walk into their lives and tell them how to organize their society. Or even how to feel about people of color. A few years forward, and it would be easier to understand that the southerners' experience of black people was more present and continuous than many of us in the north. In 2014 we have Atlanta, and we have Boston.

The outrage was also about the air of superiority we brought with us. As well as hypocrisy: the organizations we represented were hardly democratic, women were secondary in SNCC, whites were not welcome in SCLC. We were elitist utopians playing at being "of the people."

But we turned out to be at least very brave, and necessary, in pushing things forward. None who were there will ever do anything more important. We believed in the values, the culture we brought. At a certain age you believe Bach will save the world. At an advanced age you still believe it, though you admit many other realities, claims, languages.

THE BACH LITERATURE

*A*s a high school student, a college student fascinated by Bach's music, I began reading what I took to be the basic writing about him: Spitta, Schweitzer, Terry, the first edition of the *Bach Reader* with Forkel's crucial biography. I was unaware that right about that time successful research was going on about what I had already felt to be a key missing piece: an accurate chronology. The achievement of this, the work of diligent diggers using all kinds of methods ranging from old-time archival work to modern watermark and paper analysis, really helped to make sense of Bach's career.

In my early readings about Bach I had been bothered by the assumption that the so-called chorale cantatas were a later phase. They are so stylistically diverse, so much not a "group," even a beginning student of the pieces would have to be puzzled.

I was also confused and depressed by a frequent assumption that Bach in his last years was not writing for an audience, or even for performance, but instead was composing abstract musical statements—the *Art of Fugue* and the *Musical Offering*—like a lonely scientist. This is a lofty, heroic, but ultimately defeated stance, and I never wanted to accept it.

~

It is one of the many virtues of Christoph Wolff's *Bach: The Learned Musician* (Norton, 2000) that he draws from old familiar data a new and more plausible picture: Bach in the last years, discouraged and limited by many aspects of his church duties, centering more in the university—rather than sulking in his studio, puttering and revising, this is Bach in full confidence, preparing his posterity, completing his biggest projects, composing some esoteric pieces not just for his own fascination, but for like-minded, intelligent listeners, people who Christoph Wolff noticed turning up as godparents for Bach's children.

Wolff is constantly alert to factors that indicate Bach's steady sense of self-worth, the instinct that his music would go on after him. In most Bach scholarship, the Leipzig appointment is undervalued. Of course Bach was probably insulted not to be the first choice for the job, and very annoyed to be pushed out at the end of his life, but the position was a personal and family achievement, an entry into an environment that he truly sought, congenial to his artistic and intellectual ambitions. Wolff sees this in countless ways, looking beyond the many quarrels and fits of temper.

Wolff's book is an amazing combination of compact assembly of data and original thinking about what it all means. What discipline was required to pack so much information in a single volume. It will survive for many years as the basic Bach book.

~

From what I'd heard and read about it, I expected to hate Paul Elie's book *Reinventing Bach* (Farrar, Straus & Giroux, 2012). But I was grateful for it. It cheered me up a lot. For years I was worried about the diminishing presence of Bach in the teaching of music—singers in the Bach cantata at Tanglewood were typically singing their first Bach piece; string players experiencing only the solo sonata movement required for their orchestra audition; Bach, with Haydn and many formerly often-played composers, disappearing from the programs of major orchestras, having gone to live with early music.

And the cantatas, my own basic musical repertoire, even with fine advocates, many sterling recordings, still marginal. How is this possible—so many of the greatest pieces we have still the quixotic cause of specialists?

But after reading Elie's book I felt relieved. Of course his book is not about the cantatas, or the canons in the *Art of Fugue*, or the Four Duets in the third book of the *Clavier-Übung*, some of my touchstones. It is about Big Bach, Celebrity Bach, and it is a stirring, heartening tale of the grand resilience, the steady, wide reach of Bach's music, generation to generation, fuelled by a virtual relay race of colorful virtuosi, who seem to pass the flame hand to hand like Olympic runners. Going back to Schweizer, Landowska, Casals, Stokowski, on through Rosalind Tureck and Yo Yo Ma.

It makes exciting reading. I remember now the drama and surprise of Gould, this amazement of walking into friends' houses which held only one concert music recording, and finding, one of five million sold, the *Goldberg Variations*. The vivid account of those Gould recording sessions recalls the ingredients in so many of those appearances of Big Bach: a large piece, eccentricity, mystery, originality, publicity.

Elie makes a good case for believing these eruptions will always occur. The music is too convincing to ignore, it survives and even benefits from a great breadth of approaches and, like Shakespeare, it has credentials and prestige.

So I've relaxed. The cantatas are doomed to obscurity. Secularism, a natural resistance to conventional performance occasions, and a very intricate vocabulary all restrict them. But the next Celebrity Bach hero will arrive, maybe a major rock guitarist playing the complete chorale preludes of the *Orgelbüchlein*.

~

John Eliot Gardiner's *Bach: Music in the Castle of Heaven* (Knopf, 2013) has the great advantage of being written by a performer. Gardiner brings to his commentary on the choral music the same on-site view that was available to Schweitzer in writing about the organ music. He is lavish in setting the stage, first about his own up-from-the-ranks story, so typical of a British merit-system by which performers advance to leadership. A similar thoroughness guides his account of the shaping forces of Bach's career. We learn much, with profit, about Bach's uncle, Johann Christoph Bach, and his mentor Dietrich Buxtehude—the only artist in the immediate previous generation who operates in the visionary-explorative sphere soon to be further enlarged by Bach. We also get great detail about other precursors, especially Purcell and Schütz, whose direct line to Bach is difficult to trace.

Throughout his chronicle of Bach's life, Gardiner emphasizes certain qualities of temperament—quarrelsomeness, irritability, suspicion of authority—which have caused some readers discomfort. (If Bach was so irritable, so eager for dispute, how could he be the writer of such beautiful, uplifting music?) This topic is one of the most useful aspects of this book. Bach's pugnacity, simmering or erupting, has consequences for his music, and forms a central core of his life story. He finds, and eventually expects, untrustworthy, complacent, or flat-out obstructive behavior from many of the authority figures who influence his life. The repeating story is about unwavering commitment, ceaseless aspiration (no Plan B, no fallback), meeting the daily this-is-how-we-do-it, good-enough response.

It is timeless. It is re-encountered so often—even when the artist is as well-fitted for a 9-to-5, put-in-your-time mentality as was Bach.

Grateful as we may be for this useful corrective in the psychological portrayal of its subject, Gardiner's Bach is eventually diminished by the author's need to take the words of Bach's texts, the purpose of Bach's ministry, his few general statements of purpose (all of which are at base theological) as metaphorical, that is, apprendable as behavioral maxims, cautionary anecdotes, rather than what they might claim to be: rough challenges to re-magnetize your inner compass, or darkly realistic injunctions to face your inevitable fate. Calls to witness, testify, dispute, radical and impossible exhortations to attempt humility, to help the unfortunate, eleventh hour warnings to embrace Salvation. A visceral response to some or all of these exhortations at the level of what we might dare to call Belief—or at least the pain of Doubt—seems necessary, and is (dare we say) beyond the reach of the cultivated liberal aesthetic sophistication of our beleaguered twenty-first century scholars.

WHAT DO WE MAKE OF BACH?

What Do We Make of Bach?
Part I: Taking Bach's Measure

*A*long time ago I understood that the music of Bach—the first music I remember hearing—would always be present, foreground or background, in all the significant encounters of life: the chaconne, the pedal tone, heard or felt, close by.

After many years I have worn through reverence for Bach. He is so much of this world (even while his work lives in more transcendent worlds). His schnapps and tobacco, his short temper, his daily-ness, diligence, teacher's benevolence and spleen—I seek to put him to work again. Thus, I instruct myself.

Humble repeated corrections, to develop your gifts. Steady awareness of everything happening in your artistic world, anything could be useful. Balance between the inner and outer ear, between order and invention. Looking through the microscope and the telescope. Examining the slight, refined vibration, the roughest landscape.

Bach's example, his artistic level, unachieved even by the greatest Masters, even those closest—Schütz, Haydn, Mozart, Beethoven, Wagner, Stravinsky, Monk, Ellington—his Shakespearean level, needs to be noted and worn through, leaving awe, jealousy, and even gratitude behind.

If we musicians, in which I include listeners as well as practitioners, are unanimous about Bach's achievement, we should expect it can be put to use. What can we make of Bach?

We must first understand his music. This means hearing everything he wrote, then deciding which aspects to pursue, since his output, though much less in quantity than that of his contemporaries, is too vast to cover in one of our lifetimes. For myself the primary texts become the cantatas. Earlier in my study, I found that the music shared and exploited the musical grammar of its time. Against that norm it jostled but did not dislodge expectations. Hearing this requires a lively ear, to experience the precise play between the predictable and the unforeseeable. Grounded as the cantatas are in the texts of their church day with prescribed Biblical references and a very definable theology, they remain eccentric; they reveal an important peculiarity in Bach's work: he is willing to try anything from a detail on up without ever having tried it before, without ever needing it again.

At the same time we notice that in the early 1700s it was not felt to be necessary to create a novel musical language for each piece, as in our own nervous times, relieving Bach of the necessity of inventing all of his premises, leaving him free to widen and stretch his frames without having to construct them from scratch.

To keep up with Bach, through a lifetime of living near his work, we must learn and relearn to hear *his* way, from the acoustical bottom to the top, and we must aspire to track every voice in every register, in its vocal, essential integrity. The learning of even a few of his pieces this way is like a bank deposit on the work as a whole.

Bach's music does no less than create an image of the cosmos as he understood it, organized by the world of the spirit.

One of the things we notice about the musics that have arrived since Bach is a reduction of the terrain of investigation. Expressing how it feels to live, in a certain time and place, is no mean achievement. But instead of a comprehensive cosmology, it offers anecdotes, autobiography, astrology and even alchemy, it offers confessional fever charts. Much of Bach's force is in his absence from his highest flights of expression and vision, his willingness to offer them to us with no editorial or comment. His music enlists "naively" its legions of hierarchical forces, earthly and heavenly.

The more we hear Bach, the more we notice certain exemplary, useful assets:

1. A faultless understanding of the muscle power of the idea, as relates to duration of sections and movements. A ruthless and welcome control of span as it relates to materials and their forms of display.

2. Efficient and structurally lucid instrumental choices.

3. The balance of the complex and the direct. An instance: the offer of the "hook" of the chorale as tour guide through the dense terrain of the Chorale-Prelude.

4. As a contrast principle, allegiance to both the Obvious and the Recondite.

5. Effectiveness (maximizing of potential) without Effects (the manipulation and flattering of the hearer).

6. The more verdant the limbs, the more stout the trunk (clarity of harmonic spine in the most intricate of textures).

7. One single, rangy, all-encompassing, all-serving stylistic assumption, from *Matthew Passion* to *Coffee Cantata*.

8. Abundance, with no filling out, no over-feeding.

So, do we put Bach to work again? Certainly little has been accomplished by the many homage pieces, quoting the B-A-C-H motif, mobilizing dutiful, military polyphony. The fine-brushed behavior of *Ludus Tonalis*, or the many-voice textures of the European New Complexity composers, are not in conversation with Bach, nor are famous arrangements by Webern, Schoenberg, and Stravinsky (which mainly serve for a rare and awkward appearance of these composers in packaged Bach, before the standard modern symphony audience). All three of those arrangers, as composers, *have* made pieces not Bach-ish or Bach-like, but marinated, saturated, breathing it back, as in Webern's Op. 14 *Trakl Lieder*, Schoenberg's *Five Pieces for Orchestra*, No. 5, Stravinsky's *Rake's Progress*, especially Tom's aria in Act I, scene 2.

Mozart and Beethoven each made a special effort with Bach, real cost and benefit, reaching that point where they got it in their blood, Mozart resurrecting not only the texture and gist of the Lutheran Chorale-Prelude but also, amazingly, the weight of it in the Armed Men scene from *Magic Flute*. Beethoven in Op. 110 managing a rebirth of fugue in Bach's sense: flight, far from the formulaic drill the nineteenth century had found there.

It is no surprise that the best composers discover Bach in their work, digested and absorbed and finally hurled or even shitted out. Hard work and study, without reverence and awe, devouring it as food. We take it in, until we are helplessly, unwittingly, unwillingly, usefully unable to let it go.

What Do We Make of Bach?
Part II: The Deceptive Cadence

*N*ot — how do we celebrate, pay homage to, enshrine Bach. No—I wanted to write something about how we absorb and give back some qualities of our best composer in the work we do.

I wrote an essay, "Taking Bach's Measure," about the ever-present "professional" awareness of J.S. Bach. I wrote about the ones who memorized the WTC (*Well-Tempered Clavier*), or copied his fugues to inspire their own late unexpected fugues, or who started their day swallowing a devotional draft from his music.

Gathering testimony, I found that I didn't want quotation, the Berg *Violin Concerto*, the Crumb *Ancient Voices*.

And I wasn't looking for arrangements: Bach-Schoenberg, the "St. Anne" prelude and fugue; Bach-Webern, the *Musical Offering* ricercar; Bach-Stravinsky, the "Himmel Hoch" variations. Curiosities, misfortunes. Bach's music is regrettably seldom heard in programs by "big" symphony orchestras, and when it is we often get one of these misrepresentations, which are about the arrangers, even then not at their best.

The music of Schoenberg, Webern, and Stravinsky is full of real Bach: unusual opportunities and problems, accepted and solved, ambitious large spirit invoked.

If we study the score of Bach Cantata 101, we wonder how all this can sound. There are often six real parts, chromatic and jagged. The resulting harmonies are unfamiliar. There is much crossing and uncrossing of voices, with a cantus that fights to be heard through. A good description of the last movement of Schoenberg's *Five Pieces for Orchestra*: I made a piano score of that piece and played it many times, feeling "this can't work." Conducting it, some kind of miracle. Schoenberg, working in a then very unfamiliar language somehow had gauged the shape, register, and function of each line with such an accurate ear that a miracle of clarity and eventually pleasure ensues. Bach-like sovereignity over radical abundance.

Webern in the initial movement of his *Concerto for Nine Instruments*—with a texture as thin as a Bach two-voice invention, with a motivic vocabulary as sparse, with a pedagogical delight in meagerness—makes a space of play: a hearable game as joyfully frugal as a Mondrian painting.

We used to call concert music classical music, we used to call it serious music. The rubric was probably off-putting and only sometimes apt, but there are times when this music is so serious, so searching, it recalls almost at one moment everything we deem serious about life/death/love/joy/regret/wonder. Bach created many such passages. In the first movement of Cantata 105, *Herr gehe nicht ins Gericht*, as in many opening choruses in Bach cantatas, we are challenged by a kind of irresistible pressure. It is Fate, Time unstoppable; the text speaks of a day of reckoning. In *The Rake's Progress*, Stravinsky's hero faces a reckoning, a Bach cantata situation, as he begins his aria "Love Too Frequently Betrayed." Stravinsky loads up a "serious" vocabulary he has long developed for high stakes situations, as far back as his *Oedipus Rex*. Bach-fused melody and harmony, undisguised, but marinated by then in a Stravinskian stew.

This is what we must make of Bach, go right at his essence, not for a minute leave such a freighted rhetoric to the past. Hear it again as Rakewell confronts his unbearable memories in the Act I, scene 3 duet, "In a foolish dream."

Where else can we most often find ourselves in that rare territory, the majesty and comprehensiveness that Bach reaches more than all other composers?

I believe the most frequent rower in that sea (Bach the "meer," the ocean, not the brook) is Wagner. Wagner is the writer of vast tomes on many, many subjects, little of which I have read. Wagner scholars tell me mention of Bach is lacking. Where are the testimonials—in letters, conversations, pilgrimages—that we typically have from Bach's admirers throughout two centuries?

The testimonial is in the music. In no other composer do we find the diligent, inspired mastery of every compositional resource of the time. And this is based on complete command of the old chorale-based skills:

1. melody and commentary, as in the many chorale preludes embedded in *Meistersinger*;

2. reharmonization: key to the refreshing of Wagner's multiply repeated motifs;

3. development of accompaniments from primary melodies, again a chorale-fantasy requirement;

4. melody extended by the motive;

5. melody extended by unrelated material;

6. the heavily elaborated pedal point;

7. large polyphonies of multiple, equally important voices.

Isn't this what is meant by "German" music as we are asked to cherish it by Hans Sachs?

Let us remember: the oceanic surge of the first movement of the *Matthew Passion*, the immense flood occasioned by the news no ship has been seen in *Tristan*, the giant meditation on the Shepherd's melody. The ability to overwhelm, dislodge all other thoughts.

We think of Wagner's peculiar concept of voice with instruments—predominantly self-sustained, independent instrumental pieces with descanting singers, occasionally—but not typically—forming a solo/accompaniment partnership. Where else do we find this? Well, of course, it is everywhere in the Bach cantatas.

When we hear the amazing Sinfonia that begins Act III of *Meistersinger* we connect, as the composer did, with the first movement of Beethoven's C-sharp minor quartet. But its true ancestor is the Bach C-sharp minor fugue from *Well-Tempered Clavier*, Book I. This free "vocal" counterpoint, so perfectly abstract as it retells the event of the operas, it spins its motives into melodies—like the Agnus Dei of the *B Minor Mass*!

Wagner—who never tells of sitting transfixed as the Thomaschor sings "Singet dem Herrn" (his own "home" choir), who doesn't copy out fugues from the WTC as he solves the contrapuntal challenges of his late music—must have imbibed something from the Leipzig air as he walked in his youth around his home town.

BACH AND THE MODERN COMPOSER
The keynote address for the 1997 Oregon Bach Festival

*T*he most inspiring and challenging aspect of Bach for the present is his great synthesis of strict and free elements—law and fantasy—given and divined.

The mid-twentieth century gravitated to strictness, reacting perhaps to the multiplicity of discoveries around the time of World War I. Order and justification seemed necessary. More recently we see a revulsion toward rational schemes, a new musical permissiveness.

Bach's lesson is that music achieves it highest expression from a balance between the pre-ordained and the fantastic. I want to re-examine three Bachian prototypes, with special attention to their viability today: Chorale Prelude, Fugue, and Invention.

The musical history of our century is one of great arcs of action and reaction in the quest for balance between logos and ludus. Perhaps the extremity of these swings can be explained by marking the incredible variety of possibility unlocked by the musical speculations of the World War I period. Schoenberg, Debussy, Stravinsky, Sibelius, and others embarked on voyages so risky, exhilarating, destructive, and revelatory that the entire century has had its hands full dealing with them. All these composers grew up composing with one set of materials, the inheritance of European tonal and structural thinking, agreed upon for a few centuries, only to wake up in command of resources substantially of their own invention.

Stravinsky and Schoenberg both possessed very conservative temperaments, contradicting their radical instincts. Both embarked on searches for justification of their situations, Stravinsky finding it in his overt, often masklike impersonations of earlier styles (his so-called neo-classicism), most essentially a domestication of his earlier rhythm for formal purposes. Schoenberg, whose greatest innovations affected pitch, found a harbor in a method of ordering pitch sequences, a system he said assured the dominance of German music for the next century.

These systematizations, and therefore justifications of compositional processes, were more doggedly applied by students and acolytes than by the principals themselves. Especially in America, where all the major European composers had settled by the mid-forties, verifiable methods, which would certainly include the global composing method developed by Paul Hindemith, took powerful hold. When enticing intensifications of these came from Darmstadt around the same time, composition was dominated by a mania for accountability, justification, and respectability. Only the strongest, like those original Europeans, or independent-minded mavericks, survived.

During my own student days in the late '50s and early '60s, this mania for reassuring order was at its height. One alternative antidote proposal was chance, but total, complete organization and chance sounded strangely similar. It was around that time I became attracted to certain Bach pieces in which, in addition to the grounding of sturdy procedures never absent from his music, there was also a fantastical element, as in the E minor wedge organ fugue with its demonic interludes, or the fifth

Brandenburg concerto with its wacky, manic keyboard cadenza, or Cantata 10, with its fierce comedic depiction of the proud and mighty being thrown off of their chairs.

Breaking through the crust of orthodoxy was not a proposition for the timid in the '60s, and composers who start out today can have little conception of the powerful normative temper that held sway, powerful because it rested on mistaken perceptions of the work of great artists, and powerful because it proposed certain demanding technical presuppositions, hard for anyone to master, as prerequisites for membership in the guild of composers.

Remembering this unfriendly climate, I would like to honor some of my American colleagues (Europe was very little help at this point) for taking on this challenge from various perspectives—Bolcom, Crumb, Druckman, Glass, Reich, Rochberg and others who undermined, through provocative artistic statements, this glacial structure, not because of some mania for accessibility, but out of artistic necessity. Then the dam broke, the rivers ran fast. Many composers rushed toward emancipation.

In some cases it meant attempting to replace one orthodoxy with another. In other cases it suggested appeals to know-nothingism, sinister alliances between composers and listeners seeking comfort instead of illumination. By the '80s, as one of those who had lobbied for the liberation of composition from dogma and orthodoxies, I began to wish for finer standards, less pandering to easy answers, more rigor. The Bach pieces I began to seek were *The Art of the Fugue*, the four duets for keyboard, and the *Inventions*, where the element of fantasy resides in the sublime friction against the most demanding musical and philosophic propositions.

My own return to serialism, in the form of my first string quartet, coincided with the declaration of the end of serialism. I was interested in certain serial pieces like the Bach *Inventions*, where every element comes from brief motivic configurations, virtually without recourse to contrasting or transitional material. Fantasy here resides in the superb masking of this construction, fashioning this most parsimonious regimen into a seamless flow of clear, unbroken counterpoint.

Around this same time I also became interested in fugues. Bach's fugue writing contains some of his wildest and most extravagant notions, and I experimented in my second quartet with a fugue in which the countersubjects overgrow the original subject like unruly jungle vegetation, and in my second symphony with a fugue in which the subject is expressed not as a single line but in choirs of sound.

Fugue is one of the infinitely renewable strict-against-free venues for modern development. But from my perspective the richest of Bach's habitual modes is the Chorale Prelude, dating back, as it does in the earliest *cantus firmus* compositions, to the very beginnings of western music. The richness and variety of Bach's use of the chorale are hardly conceivable. It is important to remember that much of the power of these chorale compositions comes from the use of culturally significant inherited objects, the chorale tunes. To Bach's congregation they were the hymns sung in church. But even listeners who don't know the tunes can sense the importance.

In my own chorale-based pieces, I have used certain of the old Lutheran tunes that I know, I have also tried inventing chorale prototypes, and I have also tried folk songs. The quest for an analogy of the embeddedness of the chorale in the listener's psyche has led Tippett to Negro spirituals, Charles Ives to campground hymns like "Shall We Gather At the River," Frederick Rzewski to worker's songs and political rally songs.

Gregorian melodies seldom serve as Bach *cantus firmus* (with amazing exceptions like the "Confiteor" of the *B Minor Mass*) but that kind of cantus composition is very much alive in the work of Pärt, Davies, Harvey, Taverner, and Rouse.

Chorale and cantus techniques are capable of much variety, from simple harmonization of a given material to the most elaborate framing or embedding of such a material. And when we think we have encountered everything Bach might do, we run into the opening fantasy of Cantata 127, with two chorale tunes, both represented in the surrounding figuration melodies.

Invention, fugue, chorale fantasy and prelude are living principles in which Bach provides inspiration and challenge. But it is in their principle of balance between law and fantasy that their vigor resides, not in their outward framework.

Most of the music that we care about has achieved some balance of this kind. Pure play or pure rigor tend to be of the greatest interest to scholars and dilettantes. Their fusion is the essence of what we perceive to be art.

Cantata Notes

Joh Seb Bach

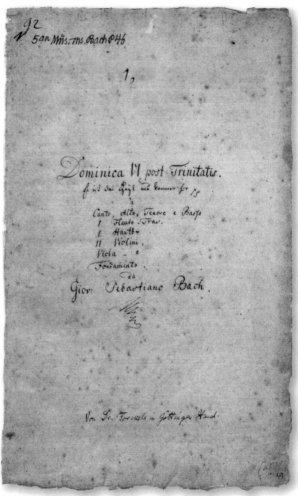

Johann Sebastian Bach. Es ist das Heil uns kommen her; V (4), Coro, orch;
BWV 9; BC A 107.   Staatsbibliothek Berlin: Mus.ms. Bach P 46 (6).

Cantata BWV 9
Es ist das Heil uns kommen her
(Now is salvation come to us)

*T*he editors of the Bach Gesellschaft Edition, the first (and often still the best) edition of Bach's compositions, decided to begin the series (in 1852) with ten church cantatas. They were asserting their conviction that the cantatas are central to Bach's enterprise. At the time of this first publication they already had examined and begun editing a large number of cantatas. Their choice of the first ten expressed the following criteria: 1) quality; 2) variety; 3) textual significance, including awareness of the major church holidays; 4) immediacy and impact. This volume of ten needed to attract subscribers and buyers—scholars, performers, libraries, and members of the small public that had heard some of Bach's music. It offered and still offers a grand tour of all the basic Bach cantata types, at a stunning artistic level.

Amid the obvious peaks of the two Easter period pieces (Cantatas 4 and 6) and the great Christmas season works (Cantatas 1 and 10), Cantata 9 at first seems light—transparent, airy, and pretty, mainly due to the charm of the opening chorus. This chorus announces the *destination* of this cantata, to be learned in the succeeding movements. It rejoices in the revelation of a certain piece of doctrine dear to Lutheranism: "Deeds can never help, they cannot protect us. Faith beholds Jesus Christ" (trans. P. Dellal). Bach and his librettist chose a hymn for the day as basis for their text. The actual lesson for the day from the Sermon on the Mount, Matthew 5:20, has a different thrust: "Unless your righteousness exceeds that of the scribes, you shall never enter the kingdom of heaven."

The gossamer sound of the opening movement disguises the fact that this cantata is the *locus classicus* of Lutheran fervor in all of Bach's work, the clearest expression in cantata form of the composer's lifelong identification with the founder of his denomination. The "story" of this cantata is Luther's story, so familiar to Bach, a progress from utter despair to hope for salvation which forms the heart of so many cantata-dramas and had personal resonance for the composer.

Luther, in a characteristic state of doubt, anguish, and torment, reads and re-reads a statement which he says he had always hated: "The justice of God is revealed in the Gospel" (Romans I:17). He ponders this for many days and nights, passionately, despairingly disturbed by his understanding that "justice" implies judgmental punishment. Here he is, in the tenor aria, the desperate sound of the low tenor voice plunging to the abyss, hectored by an avenging, distended tarantella played by the solo violin. Suddenly he sees a connection to the next of Paul's phrases, "The just shall live by faith." *Justice* acquires a connection to compassion, *faith* suggests a way through. Luther, always feeling insufficient in the world of deeds, described the effect: "I felt as if I had been born again and had entered Paradise through wide open gates. Immediately the whole of Scripture took on a new meaning for me." So we next hear the most extended vocal canon (Canon = Law) in all of Bach, the seraphic wind scoring of the first chorus returns, and two sing in the plainest folk poetry about this wonderful discovery, Luther called it a re-covery: "Nur der Glaube macht gerecht, Alles andre scheint zu schlecht" ("Only faith can justify, all the rest is just a lie," trans. J. Harbison).

Canon in Bach's generation: not only a metaphor for *law*,

something given or proved, but also a bridge to the next world, since if carried out strictly it cannot end. (But in the generation of Bach's sons, canon was regarded as the essence of old-hat, hard-disciplined, anhedonic.)

A singer in Aspen said during the coaching of this duo, "At first I thought it was the most beautiful duet I'd ever sung, but the more I sing it, our parts together, it feels very *important* and *permanent.*"

The word Gesetz (Law) appears in the first sentence of each of the three Preacher's recitations in Cantata 9. Trying to grasp the meaning of this moment in Luther's life, E.H. Harbison, in his 1958 book *The Christian Scholar in the Age of Reformation*, writes: "The only analogy that seems helpful is that of a modern scientist searching long and painfully for the answer to some question about nature, to be rewarded when all the pieces miraculously fall into place. Luther . . . was convinced that there was something *objective* about his discovery . . . The experiment could be performed by someone else. Discovery is not a revelation . . . it is a verifiable *insight.*"

This helps us to understand how Bach and his librettist could be excited to make a piece of music about doctrine. Excited enough to take it up as late as 1735, long after Bach's cantata-writing days, to substitute as text a popular hymn for the day for the lectionary lesson, to boil that hymn's sixteen verses down to fit five concise movements. Excited enough to create in the middle movements two extreme contrapuntal masterpieces—the first contorted and crazed, the second seemingly effortless—so calmly composed, it seems like a natural phenomenon.

This leads, perhaps, to reasons to present the piece at least once in translation. With all the attendant sins, mistakes, and disasters attendant upon translation, especially translation to be sung, the very possibility of catching a few words for the listener, or of making a particular kind of instinctive connection for the performer, could be useful here. Cantata 9 presents some features which, *especially* for a non-Lutheran listenership, could be easy to miss. Why are these abstract and didactic words rendered with such glowing warmth? Why did the first editions of the Bach Gesellschaft put it in their showcase Volume I? Does translation do anything to illuminate these questions?

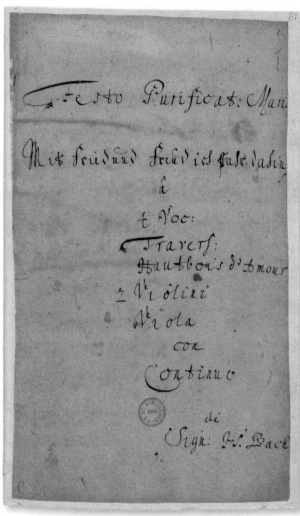

Johann Sebastian Bach. Mit Fried und Freud ich fahr dahin; V (3), Coro, orch;
BWV 125; BC A 168. Staatsbibliothek Berlin: Mus.ms. Bach St 384.

Cantata BWV 125
Mit Fried und Freud ich far dahin
(In peace and joy I now depart)

*F*irst, a grand processional chorus of nearly *St. Matthew Passion* length, seven minutes of twilight introspection, then, directly, another piece of radically similar character, an alto aria, even longer and more austere (the organist is asked to lay out, no chords).

We are reminded of the advantages to the composer (at least to one in 1725) of writing music for use in church. Principles of contrast—out the window. Limits of attention—don't worry. If Bach, in order to deliver the most profound of his five statements about Simeon in the Temple, needs to write an arduous piece, he can. This is not concert music, it does not need to divert or entertain us. It needs to guide us, illuminate us, through trial if necessary.

In much of the iconography of the scene in which Blessed Simeon after his long wait embraces the baby Jesus, the old man is depicted as blind or near-blind. This is the premise of the text of this cantata as well. Luther's hymn tune, used in the first movement, suggests (and receives in other Bach pieces) a brighter treatment, but here Bach shrouds it in mystery. Each line of text has a different melodic shape, and each reaches a distinctive musical outcome.

The alto aria, in four huge sections, similarly ignores the hopefulness we read in the text: Simeon still waits, in pain; his rescue is deferred (most wrenchingly by the instrumental outburst which interrupts the final return).

This cantata needs rescue. In the interwoven chorale and recitative for bass which comes next, it is fascinating to hear how compromised, how shadowed this revival is, again in spite of the words. Then, finally, the big tenor-bass duet arrives, a true comet of a piece—"incomprehensible light fills up the entire circle of the earth, echoing with power."

Is it enough? Luther's words in the splendid final chorale quote Simeon, in the Nunc Dimittis: "For mine eyes have seen thy salvation ... the glory of thy people Israel" (Luke II). But Bach knows also the darker part of that prophecy, spoken to Mary: "A sword shall pierce through thy own soul also."

Johann Sebastian Bach. Nur jedem das Seine; V (4), Coro, orch; BWV 163;
BC A 158. Staatsbibliothek Berlin: Mus.ms. Bach P 137.

Cantata BWV 163
Nur jedem das Seine!
(To each his own!)

*B*ach's years in Weimar saw the first great flowering of his
cantata writing. The Weimar cantatas are justly prized
for their variety, chamber-music intimacy, experimental
candor, and a strange mystical atmosphere never recalled in his
later pieces. It is fortunate that during this sojourn Bach met
and collaborated with Solomon Franck, Director of the Mint in
Weimar. Franck was the finest poet Bach set, and the cantatas
with Franck's texts benefit from his rare combination of felici-
tous, adventurous imagery, and down-to-earth subject matter.

Cantata 163 derives from a fascinating incident in Matthew 22,
a story not obviously suited to musical treatment, but nevertheless
drawing remarkable music from both Bach and his predecessor
Heinrich Schütz.

Conspiring to trick Jesus into a typically radical, seditious statement, the Pharisees ask him, "Should we be paying our taxes to
Caesar or not?" Jesus' famous answer—"Render unto Caesar
that which is Caesar's, to God that which is God's"—crossed up
and frustrated the Pharisees, and its resonance was felt by two
strongly practical visionaries in 1714 Weimar, struggling to live
in the world and reconcile it with their metaphysical longings.

The result is Cantata 163, which begins with a spare, matter-
of-fact paraphrase of Jesus' answer, sung by the tenor. Then the
bass asks the question, "Since we don't have much, what can we
give to God?" The coin will be our heart, and here the keeper
of the mint and his collaborator take us far down into this image

—the dark burnished Heart-coin (an extraordinary subterranean texture inhabited by two solo cellos). After spiraling triplets show us the shine of the coin, we enter a kind of forge where the heart is hammered into a new shape.

The final duet for soprano and alto begins with a touch of psychological realism. Even after the renewal in the forge, conviction falters: "I wanted to give you my heart but flesh and blood always resist." The extraordinarily free rhetoric of the ensuing plea for grace leads to a more formal duo-aria, the text and style of which could easily be appropriate for an operatic love duet. (The scabrous, beatific conclusion of Monteverdi's opera *Poppea* is not far removed.) Franck's text belongs in the off-center religious tradition of St. John of the Cross ("that my heart and soul stay inside you forever"). At certain points the upper strings join the soloists playing a chorale, the words of which would have been known to the Weimar congregation:

> I will not leave my Jesus
> but go always alongside him,
> Christ will lead me forever
> through the stream of life.
> Blessed, the one who tells me this –
> I will not leave my Jesus.

Bach's harmonization of the final four-voice chorale is lost, but easily reconstructed, continuing the artful simplicity of the final duet.

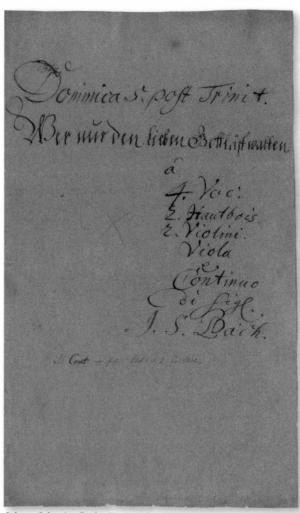

Johann Sebastian Bach. Wer nur den lieben Gott läßt walten; BWV 93.
D-LEb Thomana 93 Bach-Archiv Leipzig, Leihgabe des Thomanerchors
Leipzig. © Sammlung Bach-Archiv Leipzig.

CANTATA BWV 93
Wer nur den lieben Gott läßt walten
(Who only lets dear God rule)

*A*nyone who has willingly or unwillingly spent a day fishing learns that it requires trust and patience, or it soon evolves into boredom and anxiety. And if it is your livelihood, as it was for Peter and his companions, then constructive, hopeful waiting becomes essential. Writers and composers sometimes compare their work to fishing.

The *Siciliano* was for Bach a long familiar dance-rhythm. In choosing to suggest it in this opening chorus, he typically bends its character under the influence of the story, adding in a sense of lassitude, drifting. The piece seems to float on the lapping waves, but there is also the pull of the anchor, the chorale melody. It is important to remember that the miracle, the catch, is the Reward at the end of the lesson of waiting.

The result of that lesson of faith is the first recruitment of the disciples, the fishers of men. Just as they will eventually travel abroad with many versions of Christ's message, the chorale tune in this piece is constantly re-melodized.

The crucial turn in this piece is the line in the soprano-alto duet, "at the point when you least expect it." This is the paraphrase of the so-called "Abgesang" or concluding section of the chorale tune, here invested with a special glow and energy, the inspired movement of the Spirit.

Johann Sebastian Bach. The 'Fulde' canon in Bach's autograph (BWV 1077).
(Reproduced in *Johann Sebastian Bach: Neue Ausgabe Sämtlicher Werke* VIII/1. Bärenreiter,
1987.)

About the Author

Composer John Harbison first led Bach cantata performances in 1958 as conductor of Harvard's Bach Society Orchestra. He has continued to do so every year since then, in two tenures as music director of Boston's Cantata Singers, and as Principal Guest Conductor of Emmanuel Music for four decades (Acting Music Director from 2007-2010). Since 2015 he has been Director and Conductor for the Bach programs at Tanglewood and Songfest.

About the Editor

Sarah Schaffer, Ph.D., began her association with John and Rose Mary Harbison in 1997, when invited to manage their annual summer chamber music festival held on rural family farm property in Token Creek, Wisconsin. She became the composer's assistant soon after. Her advanced degrees in musicology and music theory are from Indiana University.

Acknowledgements

Special thanks to Andrée Valley for book layout and design, and to Ann Boyer, Zachary Preucil, and Linda Roberson for careful proof reading.